THE

BIG BOOK

OF

CALIFORNIA

GHOST STORIES

JANICE OBERDING

Globe
Pequot

Guilford, Connecticut

Globe
Pequot

An imprint of Globe Pequot, the trade division of
The Rowman & Littlefield Publishing Group, Inc.
4501 Forbes Blvd., Ste. 200
Lanham, MD 20706
www.rowman.com

Distributed by NATIONAL BOOK NETWORK

British Library Cataloguing in Publication Information available

Library of Congress Cataloging-in-Publication Data available

ISBN 978-1-4930-5862-4 (paper : alk. paper)
ISBN 978-1-4930-5863-1 (electronic)

♾™ The paper used in this publication meets the minimum requirements
of American National Standard for Information Sciences—Permanence of
Paper for Printed Library Materials, ANSI/NISO Z39.48-1992.

Contents

Central California

Southern California

Hollywood

Introduction

*I*t's true that each of the fifty states has something unique to offer visitors and residents. That said, there is no other place quite like California with its rich culturally diverse history. It's an ancient and magical place, the most populous state in the United States. This naturally includes a plethora of ghost tales, legends—and ghosts. You see, for all its natural beauty and enchanting history, California also has a sordid past; it's one of violent crime, greed, jealousy, and murder. And this all but guarantees hauntings and ghosts.

Ruled at one time by Spain and then by Mexico, Californians revolted and raised the bear flag against Mexico's rule in 1846. Statehood followed four years later in 1850 with the Golden State becoming the thirty-first state in the Union. California has been a leader ever since that time. The San Joaquin Valley provides the nation with much of its produce. But beware. Ghosts are lurking here in the Central Valley. Actually, ghosts can be found from one end of California to the other. And they bear witness to the state's darkest secrets. California's first mission, San Diego de Alcalá, was built years before the US Constitution was written and ratified. Spanish priests continued building through California in their endeavors to build a string of missions and bring religion to the native people who lived in the region. Some of them have chosen to stay on indefinitely.

The ill-fated Donner Party left Illinois for the fertile farmland of California in 1846. The following year several of the party lost their lives high in the snowbound Sierra Nevada, where they were forced to indulge in cannibalism in order to survive. Twenty-first-century visitors tell of the stillness and the eeriness of the site. That's during daylight hours. After dark, the ghosts of the tragic party become more evident.

Gold was discovered at Sutter's Mill on January 24, 1848, thus the California gold rush that brought thousands of people westward seeking their fortunes in the icy rivers and streams of Northern California.

These events, in all these places, have given rise to California's myriad legends and ghosts that roam to this day. Ghost enthusiasts, professional and armchair alike, will find the Golden State a richly rewarding location.

Northern
California

Battery Point Lighthouse

In 1845 Theophilus Magruder and James Marshall came west with an emigrant train to the Oregon Territory seeking gold. Both men were destined to play a part in California's history. James Marshall was a skilled carpenter. Theophilus Magruder's parents were socially prominent residents of Washington, DC, and he hoped to show them he could make his own wealth. It didn't happen. With the men's quest proving futile, James Marshall moved on to California where he started the California gold rush with his discovery of gold at Sutter's Mill in 1848.

Theophilus Magruder stayed in Oregon and served briefly as the state's territorial secretary in 1849. Seven years later, the lighthouse at Crescent City was completed; it began operating on December 10, 1856, with a kerosene light that could be seen from fourteen miles out. Theophilus Magruder, who had left Oregon for California, was awarded the job as the lighthouse's first keeper with a salary of one thousand dollars yearly. Three years later he resigned when his pay was cut. Although he was no longer working at the lighthouse, Theophilus remained in Crescent City.

Over the next several years, Battery Point lighthouse keepers would come and go. John Jeffrey came and stayed awhile. He arrived in 1875 with his wife and children and served as lighthouse keeper at Battery Point for the next forty years. The question is, has John Jeffrey decided to maintain a residence at the lighthouse indefinitely? Some ghost investigators believe he is the ghost whose heavy boots are often heard climbing the lighthouse stairs, or walking across the floor. Other investigators claim Theophilus Magruder is the ghostly keeper who climbs the stairs and John Jeffrey is the ghost who is accompanied by a woman and three children.

In March 1964 a 9.2 megathrust earthquake struck off the coast of Anchorage, Alaska. The most powerful earthquake ever recorded in North America, it resulted in 131 deaths. Of those, nine people died in Crescent City when twenty-foot waves came sweeping into neighborhoods. Property damage was catastrophic. And yet, the old lighthouse withstood the onslaught.

Lighthouses, like theaters, seem to be haunted by their very nature. Whoever Battery Point's ghosts are, they're known for activity like a rocking chair that will suddenly start to rock without any apparent help, the aroma of a burning cigar, and items that are moved from place to place.

Battery Point was one of California's first lighthouses. It is registered as a California Historical Landmark and is listed on the National Register of Historic Places. Visitors, with the exception of the ghostly sort, should be aware it is located on an isthmus, and is only accessible at low tide.

Truckee Hotel

*T*ruckee is a small town nestled in the Sierra one hundred miles east of Sacramento and roughly twenty-four miles from Lake Tahoe. It's a favorite summer and winter weekend getaway for those who live in the San Francisco Bay Area. With 204.3 inches of snow annually, Truckee is the fifth snowiest city in the US. That makes it perfect for skiers who flock to Lake Tahoe for fun on the slopes. Many of them come to visit the historic Truckee Hotel in downtown Truckee for its old-world elegance and ambiance. The hotel offers fine dining and music in Moody's Bistro Bar and Beats. And that leads us to a bit of hotel history that occurred on a Thursday night in late February 2003.

Former Beatle Sir Paul McCartney and his then wife Heather Mills were enjoying a ski holiday at Lake Tahoe when they came down to Truckee for a bite to eat and an evening of good music. By pre-arrangement with management, the McCartneys were incognito right up to the time Sir Paul decided to jam with the musicians. Ad-libbing, he sang a song he called the "Truckee Blues," much to the delight of everyone who happened to be in the hotel that evening.

People in Truckee still talk about that night. A once-in-a-lifetime opportunity, I wish I'd been there. I also wish I'd been at the hotel when a group of ghost investigators recorded the laughter of a little girl in the fourth-floor hallway.

In 1873 nearly a century before Sir Paul arrived at the Truckee Hotel, the original hotel was built. It was called the American House until a new owner renamed it the Whitney House in 1875. The hotel has thirty-seven rooms, some with their own private bath. Some of them are haunted, especially those on the fourth floor. The little girl ghost is believed to be that of a child who was killed in a fourth-floor room. She is sometimes seen skipping merrily down the hall. But she is not the only specter in residence. A ghostly woman dressed in a deep burgundy red evening gown, with her hair in a Gibson girl updo, is occasionally spotted in the hallways. The moment she realizes that she has been seen, the woman walks into a nearby wall and vanishes. Some say she was an early-day prostitute who was murdered outside the hotel by her lover during a violent argument. And during her final moments she sought refuge in the hotel. We may never know the truth of what leads her to haunt the Truckee Hotel, only that she does so.

Rex the Hero Dog

If people can return why can't animals? They do. In fact, there is a growing consensus among paranormal researchers that animals can and do return to the places they knew in life. According to local legend, the ghost of Rex the rescue dog continues to explore the Truckee area, especially the old Hilltop Lodge where he was kenneled. The canine ghost usually appears when the snow starts falling in the dead of winter. And in the Truckee/Donner area, snow piles up fast, making travel along the interstate all but impossible. It was even worse before the new Interstate 80 was built to traverse Donner Summit in 1964. So it was on January 13, 1952, at Yuba Pass when the streamliner train *City of San Francisco* slammed into an avalanche and was stranded atop the summit. And the snow kept falling.

Down in Truckee all that snow warmed the hearts of skiers who couldn't wait to get out on the slopes. But it was hampering rescue efforts. The train was stuck. It couldn't move forward or backward. And in the time long before the internet and news 24/7, friends and family of passengers were frantic. A doctor should go and check on their health. But how? Rex and his sled team had already proven successful in rescuing people who were snowbound in a blizzard. The Samoyed dog team was called in whenever there was a mishap. Pulling a small airplane from its crash site to a highway so it could be repaired was no easy feat. But Rex and the team did it. So it was decided that Rex would lead his team, with a doctor on board the sled, to the snowbound train. This proved to be another successful rescue mission for Rex.

The following year, Hollywood came to the Truckee/Donner area when John Wayne, cast, and crew came to film for *Island in the Sky*. Although Rex did not appear in the film, he acted as Wayne's guard dog and helped move props around the shooting site. More importantly, he made a favorable impression on John Wayne.

On snowy nights the ghostly purebred Samoyed appears at the old Hilltop Lodge with his handler; they stand a moment as if watching something, then they turn and walk through the wall. Rex has also been seen alone in other locations around Truckee. If you should hear the barking of a dog when there is no dog nearby, look for the glowing white Samoyed. Rex the hero dog may be close by. At this writing the property near the Cottonwood Restaurant is for sale with proposed townhomes and a hotel to be built upon it. When these plans come to fruition it will be interesting to see if Rex the hero dog chooses to stay in residence.

The Ghost of Juanita

*M*any years have come and gone since that terrible day on Jersey Bridge. Yet some say that on certain wintry nights just as darkness settles across Downieville, and the wind pushes low clouds over the Sierra, the lonely ghost of Juanita walks the Jersey Bridge in search of the justice that eluded her in life.

Juanita's story begins in 1848 with the discovery of gold at Sutter's Mill. Eager for adventure, the young Mexican woman persuaded her husband, Jose, that they could make a better living in the mining camps of California. So the pair traveled north from Sonora into California where thousands of men, stricken with gold fever, risked everything they held dear to pursue the sparkling yellow dust that winked just below the water's surface. At day's end they were lonely and thirsty and more than willing to part with a nugget or two.

In 1849 the quest for gold moved northward into the high Sierra and Downieville was founded. The lure of gold echoed across the canyons. Two years later the town, with over five thousand residents, was the fifth largest city in California. Juanita and Jose arrived in Downieville before winter snow piled high on the mountain trails, and soon discovered that life here was especially hard. At daybreak prospectors lined the Yuba River with their pans and their shovels. Thus occupied, they spent their days hunched over the icy waters and their nights drinking and gambling in the town's saloons.

A few found what they sought, most discovered only defeat in the raging river that tumbled across boulders and merged into the Downie. Believing that perhaps the chances of striking it rich would be better elsewhere, some men moved on. Juanita and Jose did not concern themselves with the comings and goings of the miners; when one packed up his mule and headed into the Sierra, another would soon come down out of the mountains with the glint of gold shining in his eyes.

Summer came to the mountains and the days grew longer. Patches of wildflowers colored the scraggly mountainside where trees had been felled for winter warmth. Depleted of spring run-off, the Yuba calmed. Anyone who dared to wade into the waters could do so now without fingers and toes turning to ice. It was the Fourth of July 1851 and the nation was celebrating its seventy-fifth birthday.

Those who lived in Downieville considered themselves patriotic; here was cause for celebration. On a platform festooned with red, white, and blue bunting, town leaders began the day with self-congratulatory lectures. Then the festivities moved on to carefree abandon with a parade and picnics, good natured competitions, dances, and alcohol. All in all, a jubilant day; the more jubilance the crowd shared, the thirstier everyone became.

Among the celebrants were Jack Cannan and his friends who drank more than their share of whiskey. As day faded into darkness, they headed toward their cabins. Morning would come soon enough; the gold flakes would beckon. As they strode down the dusty road on unsteady feet, the young men joked and laughed. At Juanita and Jose's tiny cabin, Cannan stumbled and crashed into the door.

Jose was dealing monte at the Craycroft Saloon; Juanita was alone in the cabin. She glared at Cannan who smiled drunkenly, stood, and brushed himself off.

Early the next day Cannan returned to the cabin. Jose met him at the door.

"I'm sorry for the—"

"Do you intend to repair our door?" Jose asked.

Cannan laughed in his face.

Jose's temper flared. "I have only asked you to do the honorable thing."

"Honor? What do you know of honor?" Cannan snarled.

Juanita stepped out from behind her husband and rebuked Cannan angrily. He had admired her beauty from the first moment he saw her. Now she was like a raging angry tigress. Maybe her husband allowed her to talk like this. He would not. Enraged, he cursed her, calling her a string of vile names.

Juanita disappeared into the shadows of the cabin; Cannan continued his tirade at the front door.

"Come into my home and say such things!" she taunted.

Cannan angrily stepped across the threshold. It was a fateful mistake. The tiny Juanita lunged at him. Too late he saw the gleaming knife she held in her hand.

"You have insulted my honor!" she screamed, thrusting her knife deep into his chest. The dying Cannan stumbled out of the cabin and onto the street. "The Mexican woman," he said to friends as he dropped to the dirt.

"Now you have done it," Jose admonished her. "Quick! We must go to Craycroft's."

While his friends carried the lifeless body of Jack Cannan to his cabin, Jose and Juanita scurried down to the Craycroft Saloon and safety. They had not reckoned on the speed with which Cannan's friends could incite the town against them.

"She has killed a good man in cold blood."

"The Mexican woman must hang!"

"Hang her. Hang her at once."

The few who called for good sense and a fair trial were quickly silenced with threats of reprisal.

Craycroft's Saloon was surrounded by thousands of angry citizens—men, women, and children—demanding Juanita. Those who had harbored her fled in fear of their own safety; now there was no sanctuary for Jose and Juanita. The angry mob rushed in and dragged them out to the town's main plaza. The pair trembled in fear. It was Juanita who had killed Cannan. And it was Juanita's blood the mob wanted.

"Get on your horse and get outta town!" an angry man told Jose.

"Pero mi esposa—"

"Your esposa is a murderess!"

Jose held firmly to Juanita's hand. "I will not leave you."

"But you must!" she said pulling her hand away. "I want you to leave at once."

He kissed her softly on the cheek. "Te amo."

"Go!" she hissed.

"I will not."

But the choice was not his to make. Several men hustled him down the street and onto his horse. Juanita was now alone; alone to face the angry mob. Her heart ached. But she would not weep and grovel before these people today. No matter what may come.

Members of the crowd appointed a judge and jury for Juanita.

"She must have a defense," a young man said, stepping up to the frightened woman. "I will be her attorney."

The mob jeered him, but reluctantly agreed. It was only right after all.

"You must not hang a woman here today. It is unthinkable," the young attorney began. "I beg you to think of your own wives, your daughters, and your mothers."

Theirs were somehow different than this young woman who stood before them. And so the attorney's words fell on deaf ears. Dr. Aiken stepped forward to add to the woman's defense.

"To hang this young woman would be reprehensible. She is with child . . . about three months. If you kill her, you will deprive an innocent child of life. Gentlemen you must not."

The crowd fell silent. Could it possibly be true? Two other doctors agreed to verify the veracity of Dr. Aiken's assertion. Juanita was led to a nearby tent where the exam proceeded. Fifteen minutes later, they emerged from the tent and announced that Dr. Aiken was lying; Juanita was not with child. The crowd pounced on the young doctor and just as they had done with Jose, they ordered him of town at once.

"Juanita you are guilty. You have one hour to prepare yourself before your hanging." With those words, the mob led her to her cabin and retreated. How she spent her final hour on earth, no one will ever know. When the citizens returned to the cabin, Juanita stepped out in her most exquisite party dress.

Her gleaming black hair was held in place with her favorite tortoise comb. Placing a wide straw hat on her head, she regally walked to her doom. She would not weep and beg them for mercy; she would hold her head high until the end. At the bridge, the noose was placed around her neck. Juanita turned and faced the crowd. Nearly all of Downieville's five thousand patriotic citizens were on hand for the hanging.

"Adios mis amigos."

And as the last rays of sunlight flickered across the water's surface, Juanita was dropped from the bridge.

On the long, cold nights of winter, some say, she returns to walk a lonely path across the Jersey Bridge. Drawn by the stories of the ghostly Juanita, my husband, Bill, and I visited Downieville last spring. But spring is often different in Downieville. Snow lay in drifts and ice was on the road. Never mind the cold, there was to be a full moon. So we checked into the inn just steps from the bridge, unpacked, and walked the town—a picturesque little gold rush town with the very ugly history of Juanita's lynching. This was not the season for tourists; most antiques stores were closed tight and so was the theater. No matter, we walked along the wooden sidewalk, shivering like the city slickers from a somewhat warmer clime that we were.

It's quiet now. But during the California gold rush millions of dollars' worth of gold was taken from this region and the world's largest gold nugget was discovered here.

Approximately 325 people live here. They are the self-sufficient sort. They don't need traffic lights, rush hour traffic, and big city noises. The availability of long lash black mascara, cat food, or a cherry chip milkshake at 3 a.m. is not important to them. Activity happening 24/7 is something people in big cities live with. It is unnecessary here, nestled in this canyon of mystery, ghosts, and legends.

One legend has Juanita sharing an unmarked grave with her victim Jack Cannan. Before it turned dark, we visited the cemetery where they're said to rest. It is an interesting old cemetery, and just in case the story is true, we paid silent respects to both Cannan and Juanita. But there is another even more macabre story.

In that tale, Juanita's skull played a starring role in the initiation ceremonies of numerous organizations. Both stories sound ludicrous. We hoped that neither was true as we made our way back to the inn where we would wait for darkness and the full moon. Then we would take cameras and voice recorders and walk the bridge, hoping for a glimpse of the ghostly Juanita.

On this night, she chose not to make an appearance. Perhaps she will deign to show up another time for us. Ghosts are like that. They have all the time in the world.

Squando, the Ghost Ship

The loud wind never reach'd the ship,
Yet now the ship moved on!
Beneath the lightning and the Moon
The dead men gave a groan.
They groan'd, they stirr'd, they all uprose,
Nor spake, nor moved their eyes;
It had been strange, even in a dream,
To have seen those dead men rise.
The helmsman steer'd, the ship moved on;
Yet never a breeze up-blew;
The mariners all 'gan work the ropes,
Where they were wont to do;
They raised their limbs like lifeless tools
We were a ghastly crew.

—Samuel Taylor Coleridge,
Rime of the Ancient Mariner

*O*ut in the San Francisco Bay just as a thick dense fog rises from the sea, a glimpse of the three-mast ghost ship *Squando* is occasionally seen from the embarcadero as she sails aimlessly around the bay. All those aboard are long dead. And yet a headless man walks the decks. He is the unfortunate first mate who fell in love with the captain's wife. If only she hadn't returned his affection. But she did. And that's where the trouble began.

It was sometime in the mid-1800s. The Norwegian ship *Squando* was docked in San Francisco. The captain had broken an old sailing rule by bringing his wife on the *Squando*'s recent voyage. Sailors held that having a woman aboard a ship was bad luck that angered sea gods and brought disastrous sailing conditions. But the voyage had been uneventful and free of disaster, except for the illicit romance between the captain's wife and the first mate.

And now the captain seethed with rage. He'd recently discovered that his wife had betrayed him in the most terrible way; she and the first mate, whom he'd once considered a friend, were involved in an affair. On her knees the errant wife begged for his forgiveness, promising to do anything he asked of her. The captain pulled her to her feet. He had an idea. He would murder the other man, with her help. She readily agreed and the plan was made.

They waited until the crew left the ship the next evening. Then she invited her lover to her cabin while her husband was preoccupied with other matters. Only he wasn't. When the unsuspecting man came to her smiling, the captain leapt from the shadows, raising an axe. His escape blocked by the woman he loved, the cornered first mate futilely raised his hands against the weapon's blows. Overhead a fortuitous thunderstorm drowned out his bloodcurdling cries as he desperately tried to dodge the axe-wielding madman. His victim decapitated, the captain dropped the bloodied axe and stared at his wife. Together, they lifted the headless man's body overboard.

From here, there are two different versions of this story. In one, the captain and his wife made their escape. And neither of them, nor the first mate's head, was ever seen again. Then there is the ending that has the captain being hanged for his crime, and his wife serving out her life in the penitentiary. Regardless, the head was never located, and the *Squando* sailed on. But thereafter the ship was cursed with some very bad luck; its next three captains all died onboard under strange circumstances. Sailors began talking about the *Squando*'s haunting.

In November 1886 the ship was wrecked in a heavy storm at Bathurst, New Brunswick, Canada. Crew members were safe and telling tales of strange doings and noises aboard the *Squando*. And nobody wanted to work on the ship's repairs. In desperation the Norwegian consul hired two watchmen for the ship.

The men were awakened when their bedclothes were pulled off and a cold, clammy hand touched their faces. "Get off this ship!" a deep and deathly voice demanded.

Fully awake, they watched helplessly as a headless man walked through their cabin, and small hand tools were tossed through the air. A small boat with four ghostly men aboard hovered over the *Squando* and seemed to disappear and reappear at will. The experience made believers of the two men who quit their jobs the next morning. From that night on, no one would stay aboard the *Squando* after dark. And then, the ghost ship began appearing out in the San Francisco Bay some 3,400 miles from Bathurst.

Alcatraz

*B*efore we leave the San Francisco Bay, let's take a look at one of California's, if not the country's, most haunted locations. Alcatraz, also known as the Rock, was used as a prison from the mid-1800s until 1963. First it was a military prison, and then in 1934 it was designated a federal prison for housing the nation's most notorious criminals. Situated in the icy waters of San Francisco Bay, and not much more than a mile from the San Francisco shore, Alcatraz was believed to be escape proof.

In its twenty-nine years as a federal prison, it would house men like Al Capone, Robert Stroud (the Birdman of Alcatraz), Machine Gun Kelley, Alvin Karpis, James "Whitey" Bulger, and Arthur Barker. It wasn't a pleasant experience. Nor was it meant to be. Many of the inmates, who were fortunate enough to leave the Rock for other facilities or freedom, complained of Alcatraz's incessant cold that could chill a man to the bone.

Inmate Roy Gardner, known as the Last Great American Train Robber, called Alcatraz the toughest, hardest place in the world. In his autobiography titled *Hellcatraz*, Gardner told of his interactions with other inmates and the harsh conditions of the prison. He didn't exaggerate. And one thing is certain, no one escaped. Well, there was the attempt made by Clarence and John Anglin and their pal Frank Morris who made an escape in a raft fashioned of tarps and raincoats.

On June 11, 1962, into the icy waters went the makeshift raft carrying the three men. They were never recaptured, their bodies were never found, and on December 31, 1979, the FBI closed the case, saying the men had most likely drowned. But did they? For many years afterward stories of sightings of the three convicts were reported.

The first time I saw Alcatraz it was still being used as a federal prison. My family and I were aboard one of the red and white fleet ferries that cruise around San Francisco Bay. The boat was not permitted to get within hundreds of yards of the prison. And so we circled the Rock, all the while a tour guide detailing some of the infamous killers who resided there. My childish imagination running rampant, I shuddered, never dreaming that one day I, too, would spend a night on Alcatraz.

Fast forward forty years and there I was spending the night on Alcatraz with a small group of friends and fellow ghost investigators. It was raining intermittently. And yes, it was cold. But what struck me was how close San Francisco was. We followed our tour guide as he led us to the small landing where Arthur Barker and four pals tried to make an escape on January 13, 1939. For his trouble Barker was shot dead by prison guards. The other four men were taken to solitary confinement. On stormy nights it's said that the failed escape attempt of Barker and his buddies can still be heard there on the beach.

We continued our foray through the cellblock and into the Birdman Robert Stroud's cell and that of Al Capone. Our guide pointed out bullet holes fired by guards in their effort to quell rioting. And then after reminding us of the rules, he bid us good evening and we were on our own. The boat left the island for the night and no one was coming or going . . . until morning.

First thought: If Alcatraz is so terrible why is it haunted? Wouldn't death ensure the freedom to leave the Rock forever? You would think so, and yet Alcatraz *is* haunted. One of the strangest stories takes place in Cell 14D. An inmate who was confined there in the 1940s began screaming one night about being killed by a monster with red glowing eyes. The next day he was discovered strangled in his cell. His killer was never discovered. For weeks after his death, guards taking roll would report seeing his ghost line up with the other convicts, only to vanish after the count was made.

According to ghost investigators who've spent time in the cell, it is occupied by a dark and negative force that especially enjoys taunting women. They also point out that the cell is colder than other areas of the cellblock. Another resident of cellblock D was the bloodthirsty bootlegger Al Capone, aka Scarface, who rose to prominence during Prohibition. To keep boredom at bay, Capone took up playing the banjo while locked away on the Rock. He was so good that he was permitted to join the inmate band. Listen! Over the years guards and visitors alike have reportedly heard the ghostly Al Capone strumming his banjo.

Robert Stroud, the Birdman of Alcatraz, is yet another ghostly resident of cellblock D. Stroud was portrayed as so caring and compassionate toward birds, that he became a didactic ornithologist in the 1962 film *Birdman of Alcatraz* starring Burt Lancaster. It is largely fictional, claim guards and historians, who've written that Stroud was brutal and anything but kind.

A ghost investigator recorded a man's voice uttering some very foul language near Stroud's cell at Alcatraz. Was it Stroud? Who can say? And who can say why a ghost would choose to say confined to a prison he so wanted to escape from in life?

The Ghost of Twin Peaks Tunnel

*A*modern marvel, San Francisco's Twin Peaks Tunnel celebrated its inaugural run on New Year's Eve 1917. Slightly more than two miles in length, the tunnel was the longest railway traffic tunnel in the world at that time. This progress did not come without loss.

Those who helped build the tunnel faced constant danger. An inspector was electrocuted in the tunnel and another man was killed during a cave-in that injured three other men. In 1917 Joseph Santi, Michael Gallagher, and Louis Fouseco lost their lives in a horrific explosion while investigating a faulty blasting cap. Fouseco was severely injured, the newspaper reporting that his eyes had been blown out and his chest was crushed. It was believed that some of those who were killed in these accidents may have decided to stay on and haunt the tunnel.

The March 10, 1920, issue of the *San Francisco Call* carried the story of several conductors on the municipal railway cars who insisted that at least one ghost was haunting the tunnel. What's more, they said, this ghostly man had the ability to whistle a tune loud and clear as he stalked the tunnel.

Some conductors had not only heard him whistling, they had seen him as well. The ghost, they explained, vanished into thin air when he realized he'd been spotted. That was a hundred years ago, but it is something to think about when you next ride Muni.

Hewlett Tarr: The Man in the Mirror at the Curran San Francisco

*T*rying to break a monopoly held by an enterprise that controlled much of New York's theaters, brothers Lee and Jacob Shubert began building theaters across the United States. The Shuberts were creating a successful organization; they knew and understood theater. They also knew a great city when they saw one.

In San Francisco the Shuberts formed a partnership with West Coast theatrical producer Homer Curran who owned a small theater known as the Curran. This would not do for the Shuberts' plans. In 1921 they bankrolled the entire building of a newer and grander theater on Geary Street. The new Curran Theater would open its doors in September 1922. With marble floors and crystal chandeliers, the Curran Theater was impressive. The Shuberts quickly dubbed San Francisco the hub of West Coast theater.

Most people who've seen the 1950 classic *All About Eve* probably don't realize that the scenes of the interior and exterior of a Broadway theater were actually filmed at the Curran Theater. Most people probably don't realize that the historic theater is haunted. But what is a theater without a ghost?

Ghosts are ubiquitous to theaters. Usually it's the specters of long-ago actors and actresses, who loved the stage and the audience's admiration so much, they refused to exit stage left—or right for that matter. The ghostly man in the mirror at the historic Curran Theater on Geary Street in San Francisco has a different reason for sticking around the premises.

On November 28, 1933, twenty-five-year-old Hewlett Tarr had been with the Curran Theater for seven years. He loved his job, and he was good at it. As he stepped into the box office and greeted theatergoers eager to see the next performance of *Showboat*, Tarr may have thought of Dorothy, his fiancée, who would be his wife in a matter of weeks. He might even have smiled as the last of ticket purchasers moved away from the booth. He would soon be meeting Dorothy at a nearby café for dinner.

But fate changed his plans. A man of about his same age, scraggily and glaring with pitiless eyes, stepped up to the booth.

"Give me all the money," he demanded, placing his gun through the opening. Hewlett Tarr was stunned. Before he could react, the man fired his gun without warning, striking him in the chest. As Tarr stumbled from the box office, his killer ran through the crowded theater and out the door. It would be two weeks before he was captured.

Eddie Anderson readily admitted to shooting Hewlett Tarr but insisted he hadn't meant to kill him. "I didn't intend to shoot Tarr. I was nervous. My gun got caught in the box office grille and it was discharged accidently."

He confessed to committing a string of stick ups but only wanted the money so he could squire his girlfriend around San Francisco in the style she wanted to be accustomed to. Eddie Anderson pleaded not guilty. Eleven days after murdering Tarr, he was convicted and sentenced to be executed at San Quentin. On February 15, 1935, he was hanged at the San Quentin prison gallows.

Our story doesn't end there. As the shock of losing a valued employee to violence wore off, the theater continued offering theatergoers off-Broadway productions. And then one night a patron glanced into the antique mirror for a quick check of her coiffure. Instead of her own reflection, the woman was startled to see the image of a man staring back at her. Who was the man in the mirror and what did it mean? She didn't say a word. But others soon noticed the ghostly man who appeared in the mirror.

When called upon to witness the strange phenomenon, theater employees knew exactly who it was. Patrons who kept abreast of current events also had an idea about the ghostly man's identity. Apparently, Hewlett Tarr had not left the theater after all. Death dashed his plans of living happily ever after with the lovely Dorothy, so what else could he do? He has chosen to stay on and haunt the Curran Theater that he loved so much.

Think of all the performances that have taken place in that time. And think of all the entertainers, people like Katharine Hepburn, Isadora Duncan, and Edith Piaf, that have trodden the boards of the Curran, and of all the people who will in the future. No wonder the ghost of Hewlett Tarr remains on the premises.

Mark Twain and the Kearney Street Ghost

By all accounts, writer Mark Twain was not a big believer in the paranormal, particularly ghosts. The story he wrote for the January 1866 issue of the *Territorial Enterprise* in Virginia City, Nevada, concerns a family and its ghost problem. Most likely the source of this story is Twain's vivid imagination. Nonetheless it is part of California's rich ghost heritage, and so I've included it.

According to Twain, the Albert Krum family, who lived in a mansion on Kearney Street in San Francisco, was having great difficulty keeping hired help. It seems a hateful ghost also resided in that mansion on Kearney Street. And he disrupted each new housekeeper's sleep until the poor candidates had no choice but to quit.

No matter what the Krums did, the trouble continued with the nasty spirit chasing off one housekeeper after another. The story ends with the ghost bringing nine kittens to the bedside of Krum's wife. One by one the moaning ghost placed the kittens on her pillowcase, leaving bloody handprints on the helpless kitties.

Twain closed his story by asking, *What do you think of that? What would you think of a ghost that came to your bedside at dead of night and had kittens?*

Neptune Society Columbarium

San Francisco is a city without cemeteries. However, there are three exceptions: the defunct Mission Dolores Cemetery and the San Francisco National Cemetery at The Presidio. And then there is the Neptune Society's Columbarium in which the cremains of an estimated thirty thousand former San Francisco residents are kept in urns and niches. Among those who rest here are actor Roddy McDowell; Harvey Milk, the first openly gay man elected to a public office in California; Dante the Magician (Harry August Jansen); and Jose Santana, father of Carlos Santana.

The columbarium was built in 1898 as part of the Odd Fellows Cemetery. When the city banned burials and the sale of cemetery lots in 1900 with Ordinance 8108, bodies were exhumed and moved elsewhere. And the cemetery was abandoned. Ten years later cremation was also banned. The crematorium, along with several mausoleums, was then demolished and over the years the columbarium fell into disrepair.

In 1980 the Neptune Society bought the building and began restoration. Today it is one of San Francisco's more obscure points of interest. Nonetheless it is well worth a visit. Right there in the midst of a quiet residential neighborhood, the columbarium's architecture and history alone make it worth a visit. Some niches hold urns along with keepsakes, treasures, and mementos of those whose ashes rest within. Then, too, there are the ghosts. Even during the quietest of times, the occasional sound of ghostly footsteps echo through the columbarium, reminding us that the dead really are only in the next room.

A little girl who likes to follow visitors is the most often reported ghost in residence. Legend has it that the child was Viola von Staden, the victim of the city's deadly 1906 earthquake. If little Viola sees that you've noticed her, be prepared; the little ghost girl is not shy about taking someone's hand and holding onto it firmly. There is also the story of a woman who happened to be wearing a dark colored jacket when she visited the columbarium. Imagine her surprise when the ghost tapped her on the shoulder as she sat in deep thought. This was probably nothing compared to her reaction when she discoved the small white handprint on the shoulder of her jacket.

USS *Hornet*

*T*he USS *Hornet* is billed as one of the most haunted places in America for good reason. It is. And anyone who is the least bit sensitive to ghosts and otherworldly activity will feel this the moment they walk up the gangplank.

The *Hornet*, the eighth US Navy battleship to bear the name, is permanently docked at Pier 3 at the decomissioned Alameda Naval Base. Commissioned in 1943, the *Hornet* saw battle during World War II and was one of the Navy's most decorated ships. But the aircraft carrier is most noted for having been selected by the Navy in 1969 to be the prime recovery ship for *Apollo 11*, the US's first lunar landing mission. Among dignitaries onboard for the historic July 24, 1969, splashdown were President Richard Nixon and Admiral John S. McCain. That's the bright side.

On the not so bright side, over three hundred men lost their lives on the USS *Hornet*. Some of them may be the spectral sailors that have been seen throughout the ship. I didn't see a ghost when I took part in an overnight ghost hunt of the USS *Hornet* several years ago, but I heard one.

On this night the hospital seemed to be the most active spot onboard. Those who recorded EVP (electronic voice phenomena) were thrilled to be receiving Class A EVP. And then someone started following a sailor only to have him turn and vanish before her startled eyes. After the early night investigation, we turned in. Yes, we were sleeping in sailor's berths (like hammocks.) We were told to stay put and not to go exploring.

Okay with me, except I'd forgotten my blanket and had to make do with a sweater. This was truly roughing it; there were no sheets and no pillowcases on the beds. *But what's one night*, I told myself, crawling into a bunk. I listened to the sound of snoring all around me, as I tried to fall asleep in the most uncomfortable bed I'd ever endured. Just as I was on the edge of sleep I heard a voice say, "This isn't how we did it."

Assuming it was one of the other investigators defiantly setting out to explore the ship, I closed my eyes and fell asleep. But it wasn't peaceful. I tossed and turned all night long with the incessant knocking and banging going on. *The sailor's life was not one of creature comforts*, I told myself, shivering in the cold. The sweater I was using for warmth kept falling to the floor. The next morning my sweater was nowhere to be found.

Over breakfast one of our guides said the noise is commonplace. They all assume it's just one of the ghosts. And my sweater? "Things sometimes do disappear here on the *Hornet*," he told us. But what would a long dead sailor want with my red sweater?

The Ghost of William Roe and the Napa Courthouse

On the morning of January 16, 1897, convicted murderer William Roe was led from his cell to the jail yard of the Napa Courthouse. Today he was to pay for the cruel murder of Lucinda Greenwood during a home invasion of the Greenwood farmhouse on February 10, 1891. Roe had forced chloroform upon John and Lucinda Greenwood so that he and an accomplice could toss the farmhouse in search of money and valuables. John Greenwood survived the ordeal; Lucinda didn't.

According to the January 16, 1897, edition of the *Sacramento Record Union*, the condemned man mounted the scaffold and Sheriff McKenzie asked if he had any last words. Roe looked around at the crowd.

"I haven't much to say, only my thanks for the way I've been treated. The sheriff and all the officers have treated me well. I have got no creed, nor kin, nor anything like that. I think that is all."

He acknowledged a friend with, "Hi Jack, my good boy" as the noose was dropped around his neck.

"Be quick and see that the noose is tight," Roe admonished Sheriff McKenzie.

It was. And the sheriff didn't waste another moment. He raised his right arm and gave the signal. Roe dropped to his death, marking the last public execution in the state of California. But it wasn't the last of William Roe.

His angry ghost has been spotted in the area of his execution and the courthouse many times over the years. But where are his mortal remains? Legend has it that Roe donated his body to science. Somehow it fell into the hands of a doctor who took it to his laboratory where he bleached the bones and reassembled the skeleton. Rather than burying Roe's remains, the doctor used the skeleton as a teaching aid in anatomy classes. And then the skeleton vanished. Perhaps this is why the ghostly Roe appears to be so agitated.

Donner Party Ghosts

*E*ach year thousands of tourists visit Donner Memorial State Park outside the small town of Truckee. Just under a hundred miles east of Sacramento, the park is the perfect place to get away for a day or a weekend. Amidst tall pine trees on the edge of Donner Lake in the Sierra Nevada Mountains, Donner Memorial State Park offers boating, fishing, hiking picknicking, and camping. It's all very picturesque and idyllic, but make no mistake, the park has a dark history. It's a history that includes unimaginable suffering, hopelessness, and—cannibalism.

Our story begins in the spring of 1846 when the Donner Party left Springfield, Illinois. In the wagon train were eighty-seven people, each with their own dreams of just how wonderful life would be in California; none of them could have imagined the horror that awaited in California's Sierra Nevada Mountains.

The first mistake came when the party leaders, eager to get to California, made a fateful decision in choosing a new and untested route known as the Hastings Cutoff. The route was difficult and dangerous, causing the loss of water, valuable livestock, wagons, and time. This set them back thirty days. They would have to make it over the mountains before winter set in and snow started falling.

But once they reached present-day Reno, they were fooled by the balmy early fall weather. They set up camp and let the days go by. Finally in late October the Donner Party pulled out, heading for the Sierra Nevada and the last leg of their journey.

They'd barely started to cross the mountain range when an early fall snow storm blew in from the northwest. A broken axle on George Donner's lead wagon forced him to stop and attempt repairs. At his urging the other wagons rolled on. He and his wife, Tamsen, and their children would make camp here. The snow began to pile up.

Six miles from the Donner's camp the other wagons were trapped in deep snow and forced to stop. There was nothing else to do. They would make camp here until it stopped snowing. But it didn't. The snow kept falling, all through the night and into the next day. As days turned to weeks, the food supplies dwindled. Hunting was impossible in snow that stood in drifts twelve feet high.

In desperation they slaughtered their animals. As hunger set in again, they made soup from the bones and finally from the leather of their shoes, shoelaces, and book bindings. When everything that could be eaten had been eaten, they turned to cannibalism. If anything might lead to a haunting, cannibalism surely would.

Among the ghost sightings at Donner Memorial Park is the glowing woman who's been seen throughout the park. She is usually spotted around the campgrounds area, and has been known to appear in the tents of startled campers. Some believe she is the ghost of Tamsen Donner, wife of George Donner. When he died, Tamsen and her children made the six-mile trek to the main camp. In the spring rescuers came and took all the survivors over the mountains to California. Tamsen was too sick and weak to make the trip, so she sent her children on with the other survivors, promising to come to them when rescuers returned for her later that year.

Now there were only two people left behind at the campsite: Tamsen Donner and Lewis Keseberg, who was unable to travel due to a recent injury. What happened after that is still a mystery. When a rescue party returned for them only Keseberg was alive. There was no sign of Tamsen Donner. However, Keseberg was frying a pan of human flesh that he claimed was that of Tamsen Donner.

She had fallen into the creek one night and died the next morning, according to Keseberg. He admitted to cannibalizing her, but insisted he hadn't murdered her. Although he was eventually cleared of murdering Tamsen Donner, suspicion and repulsion would follow him the rest of his life.

When drinking years later, Keseberg reportedly claimed that Tamsen Donner's liver tasted better than California beef. He is also quoted as having told C. F. McGlashan, author of *History of the Donner Party,* "The flesh of starved beings contains little nutriment. It is like feeding straw to horses. I cannot describe the unutterable repugnance with which I tasted the first mouthful of flesh. There is an instict in our nature that revolts at the thought of touching, much less eating, a corpse. It makes my blood curdle to think of it!"

Some believe that Lewis Keseberg is the ghostly bearded man who has been seen in and around the Emigrant Trail Museum at the Donner Memorial State Park. And that he is responsible for the cold spots felt throughout the building. The ghosts of those who were cannibalized are said to roam the park as well. They stay near the large boulder that bears the names of survivors and those who perished in the long-ago winter of 1847. Depending on which historian is consulted, the bodies of those who died were either buried in this area or near the pioneer monument.

"Indeed, if I do not experience something far worse than I have yet done, I shall say the trouble is all in getting started."

—TAMSEN DONNER, 1846

Queen Anne Hotel

The Queen Anne Hotel didn't start off as a hotel when it was built in 1890. It was an exclusive girls' school for the daughters of San Francisco's crème de la crème. The school on the corner of Sutter and Ocatavia was befitting such wealth with its thirty-one elegantly appointed private bedrooms. Miss Mary Lake was the school's headmistress. How she afforded to own such a fine school is a question San Franciscans asked themselves.

Miss Lake's family had money, but not enough to have financed such a school. Millionaire James Fair had taken care of the expenses. Fair had struck it rich in Virginia City's silver lode, served as a Nevada state senator for one term, and then moved to San Francisco. Fair was a ladies' man, a philandering husband whose wife divorced him for adultery in 1884. It was said that Fair wanted the school built so that his own daughters would not have to leave the city in order to get a good education.

Or was there a romance between Fair and Mary Lake, as gossip hinted? Both Mary Lake and James Fair denied the rumors. And to their credit they were never caught together in a situation that would lead anyone to believe otherwise. Still the rumors persisted, even as the Miss Mary Lake School for Girls became San Francisco's most prestigous school.

In 1894 James Fair died, leaving the school to his daughters who ordered it closed down two years later. In 1899 the building was sold and over the years changed hands numerous times. In 1902 Mary Lake moved to New Jersey and died there in 1904. But that isn't to say that she may not have returned to the building. The Queen Anne Hotel is the latest incarnation of the former Miss Mary Lake School for Girls. And since its inception in the late 1980s, the hotel has experienced ghostly activity.

The ghost is believed to be that of Miss Mary Lake because most of the activity takes place in her former office suite, Room 410. She's a kind and considerate ghost who's been known to throw an extra blanket on a guest on a particularly chilly night. Some who've stayed in 410—and why would a ghost enthusiast stay in any other room—claim the friendly spirit has even assisted them in unpacking. Others have reported hearing the sound of little girls' laughter throughout the old building.

During a paranormal conference in which I was a speaker, I had the opportunity to investigate the Queen Anne. It was a cold and rainy San Francisco night and my daughter-in-law and I spent it seeking ghosts in various areas of the hotel. In the predawn hours we concluded the investigation, convinced that there were indeed ghostly children on the premises. As we started up the stairs from the second to the third floor, I heard distinct giggling and stopped to take photos of the stairs. Following the rule of three, which is three photos one after the other, I got my shots. The resulting three photos were amazing. They seemed to show something etheral forming and going up the staircase. I don't believe it was Miss Mary Lake, but rather long-ago students of the school.

My friend who stayed in Room 410 didn't sleep a wink. Something scraped against the fireplace all night long, she told us the next morning. And although she didn't feel frightened or uneasy in any way, she also told us that she would never, and she stressed the word never, stay in Mary Lake's suite again. Yes, that makes her a bit of an oddity as far as ghost hunters go. Most prefer the haunted room.

The Mysterious Mary Ellen Pleasant

*A*cross the street from the Queen Anne Hotel on the corner of Octavia and Bush Streets is the Mary Ellen Pleasant Memorial Park, where Mary Ellen Pleasant's thirty-room mansion once stood. Tall eucalyptus trees adorn the area, trees that Pleasant planted herself over 150 years ago. If you happen to stand beneath one of them, speak kindly of Ms. Pleasant. Her ghost is said to hurl eucalyptus nuts down upon anyone who dares to do otherwise. But this isn't the extent of the ghostly Pleasant's repertoire of paranormal mischief. She can cause the air to take on an icy chill any time, day or night, and appear ominously in the flesh when angered.

There are many variations as to where Mary Ellen Pleasant was actually born. According to one, she was born in New Orleans in 1814 and was raised in Massachusetts where she worked for an abolitionist family. There the beautiful Mary Ellen caught the eye of a weathly plantation owner and abolitionist, and together they worked to ensure the safety of runaway slaves.

With the end of the Civil War, she worked tirelessly for the benefit of the black community and continued to do so throughout her life. Still, much of her life is shrouded in mystery. Some of this is due to the many variations and stories she told of her life.

One story has her husband, John James Pleasant, dying early in the marriage and the widowed Mary Ellen packing up and moving to San Francisco. Another has him very much alive and sharing in her wealth. But it is in San Francisco where the mysteries begin. It was said that Mary Ellen Pleasant rose to power in a time when women seldom did because she was related by marriage to Marie Laveau, the notorious New Orleans Voodoo Queen. And thus Mary Ellen was instructed in voodoo magic and had its power behind her. She certainly may have.

But let's not forget that Mary Ellen Pleasant was also one of this country's first black millionaires. She invested her money wisely, and helped to create the Bank of California. She has also been referred to as the Mother of Civil Rights in California. She didn't spend all her time in her mansion. She was an early-day activist for her people. When she didn't like the way she, or a member of her race, was being treated, Mary Ellen Pleasant wasted no time in bringing lawsuits to change things.

Among her friends were the city's wealthiest power brokers. One of them was Thomas Bell and his wife, Teresa. The Bells lived with Pleasant in her palatial home that was known as the House of Mystery. It was whispered that Thomas Bell and Mary Ellen Pleasant were actually lovers, and the marriage to Teresa a sham. In 1892 when Thomas Bell died from a fall from the stairs, some thought Mary Ellen had murdered him with the help of Teresa Bell. Since there was no proof the rumors remained as dead as Thomas Bell himself.

And then Teresa Bell got greedy. Instead of sharing Bell's fortune with her longtime friend Mary Ellen Pleasant, the ungrateful Teresa wanted it all. The battle ended up in court and not surprising Mary Ellen lost. She was tossed out of her mansion with barely more than the clothes on her back.

She died in 1904 at the age of eighty-nine. But that wasn't the end. Her mansion was eventually converted to a boarding house; those who lived there claimed to have encountered Mary Ellen in different locations of the house. Her grim ghost, they said, was always in a disagreeable mood. Anyone who dared have a kind word for Teresa Bell could expect the wrath of ghostly Mary Ellen Pleasant.

Today the Mary Ellen Pleasant Memorial Park and Green Eye Medical Group (hospital) stand at the site of the Mary Ellen Pleasant/Thomas Bell mansion. And there are those ecualyptus trees, that legend says were planted by Ms. Pleasant herself. Say only kind words of the woman who once lived here, lest you want to face a torrent of eucalyptus nuts and an angry and very ghostly old woman.

Dashiell Hammett Party of One (John's Grill)

*J*ohn's Grill has been a San Francisco landmark for over a century. The list of celebrities who've dined at the restaurant is extensive and includes people like Luciano Pavarotti, Bill Gates, Ronald Reagan, Johnny Depp, Robin Williams, and Lauren Bacall. But one patron has decided to remain on the premises even after death— author Dashiell Hammett. Hammett was the author of hardboiled detective novels that were a popular genre from the Roaring Twenties until the 1930s. Perhaps Hammett's most popular book was his 1931 *The Maltese Falcon.* Ten years later *The Maltese Falcon* hit the silver screen starring Humphrey Bogart, Mary Astor, and Sydney Greenstreet. It was an instant film noir success. And this is where we enter John's Grill.

The restaurant was one of Dashiell Hammett's favorites. He was often spotted dining alone or occasionally with his wife, playwright Lillian Hellman. John's Grill at 63 Ellis Street is just over a half a mile from Hammett's own apartment on 891 Post Street, within walking distance and the perfect hangout for an author. It's said that Hammett wrote much of *The Maltese Falcon* right here at John's Grill while feasting on a favorite dish. Indeed, his namesake dish is the lamb chops.

Look around. Photos of Hammett and other celebrities adorn the walls. Just to keep it authentic the bar offers up a number of libations including Hammett's Classic Martini and Spade's Manhattan. Then, too, there is the replica of the mysterious Maltese Falcon encased in the dining room on the second floor known as—you guessed it—the Maltese Falcon Room.

But why let death end a perfectly good habit? Dashiell Hammett certainly hasn't. He's said to frequent John's Grill. Countless people have seen him at the restaurant since the day he died in January 1961. One woman swore she'd seen a real flesh-and-blood man sitting alone at a table sipping a martini. What caught her eye was that the gent was dressed in rather outdated garb. He seemed to be deep in thought, and she had no reason to believe he was a ghost—until he vanished before her startled eyes.

Moss Beach Distillery

*I*n 2007 while filming its fourth season, the popular ghost hunting TV show *Ghost Hunters* (The Atlantic Paranormal Society or TAPS) visited Moss Beach Distillery at Half Moon Bay to film episode eleven. The resulting show that aired on June 4, 2008, was a cause for celebration in the paranormal for a time. Apparently, the show's two stars, Jason Hawes and Grant Wilson, felt the distillery should have told them about the special effects in the restaurant. There were hard feelings all around, and TAPS left not knowing if the place was haunted or not.

In 1992 psychic medium Sylvia Browne was invited to the restaurant to see if she could find the identity of the ghost that haunted the establishment. Browne determined that her name was either Mary Ann or Mary Ellen Morley. The ghostly woman, according to Ms. Browne, was dressed in blue from head to toe. Thus, she became known as the Blue Lady.

Famed parapsychologist, magician, and writer Loyd Auerbach wrote an article in which he vouched for the restaurant's haunted authenticity. He'd done research, events, and investigations at the distillery and knew the restaurant's ghostly activity was real. In fact, the ghostly Blue Lady of the Moss Beach Distillery had been featured in the October 28, 1992, episode of Robert Stack's *Unsolved Mysteries*.

But Jason Hawes, Grant Wilson, and team were not happy with what they discovered during an investigation. In the ladies' bathroom there is a blue face in the mirror. It is obviously a gag; doubtful that anyone past the age of twelve would believe she is seeing a real ghost when looking in this mirror. Fake, they claimed. Yes, it is.

They were convinced when they climbed into the attic to discover that the hanging lamps that move mysteriously were on a timer. So is the Blue Lady ghost real? There have been reports of ghostly activity at the Moss Beach Distillery from the 1930s. The Blue Lady's story is perhaps the saddest of all stories that surround the distillery.

When he came upon it, Frank Torres knew this was the perfect spot for a speakeasy. Overlooking the beach on a quiet road, it had easy beach access and was secluded, but not so much that customers couldn't find it. So he built his Frank's Place here at the height of Prohibition. Catering to celebrities and other wealthy clientele, Torres made a lot of money. Prohibition was repealed in 1933 and Torres continued to run a profitable business. His restaurant was that good. Entertaining in the bar was a handsome piano player who caught the eye of a beautiful, but married, young woman.

She sneaked out every night just to be near him. One evening they were walking arm in arm on the nearby beach when an unknown assailant shot and killed her. And she has haunted the restaurant ever since. Blue was her favorite color, the color she always wore. She is known as the Blue Lady because she always appears in blue whenever she is spotted on the beach or at the restaurant. That's one story.

Another has her driving a car down Highway 1 when she swerved to avoid something in the roadway. She was killed instantly. Her lover survived. And yes, she was wearing blue. So she made the short trip from Highway 1 to the Moss Beach Distillery, and has haunted the restaurant ever since. She sometimes makes her presence known by calling employees by name when they are alone in the restaurant. If she particularly likes a woman's earrings, she has been known to take one as a souvenir. Eventually the earring turns up. The Blue Lady plays with the lights, not those on the timer! She also likes to move things around and locks doors, all as a way of saying, "Here I am."

The patio at the Moss Beach Distillery offers a wonderful dining experience. And doggies are welcome. On a cooler than normal day, blankets are provided for those who want one. Just remember that on these grey days, as a fine mist rolls in off the bay, you're liable to see the ghostly Blue Lady walking forlornly along the beach.

I visited the Moss Beach Distillery with EVP specialists Mark and Debby Constantino shortly before the Ghost Hunters visited.

Because we'd heard about the ghost in the mirror, Debby and I headed to the *haunted* ladies' room. Obviously, the face in the mirror was phony. Nonetheless, we checked our makeup, took photos, and attempted to record EVP. Fake face in the mirror or not, we both came to the conclusion there was at least one *real* ghost inhabiting the ladies' room.

And that's something I've never understood. Why do ghosts haunt bathrooms? Lucky for us it was a slow day at the restaurant and we were allowed to explore at our leisure. After, we grabbed blankets and sat out on the patio, sipping wine and contemplating the ghostly Blue Lady and just when she might choose to make another appearance.

The Ghost Lady of Stow Lake

*I*t is one of San Francisco's oldest ghost stories. The haunting is said to occur in one of the most beautiful city parks in the US, Golden Gate Park.

There is so much to see and do in this park that covers over a thousand acres. There are hundreds of flowers and trees, the Japanese Tea Garden, the de Young Museum, botanical gardens, California Academy of Sciences, the Bison Paddock, and Stow Lake. The manmade lake features a waterfall and old-fashioned bridge and a small island known as Strawberry Island. Rent a boat and enjoy the pastoral setting, the water, the trees, and on occasion—the ghost lady of Stow Lake.

As it is with many ghost stories, there's an explanation as to why she haunts the lake. In one story she was a young mother in the early 1900s. During a visit to the park she stopped to chat with a friend. While she visited with her friend, her child wandered into the lake and was drowned. The death of her child drove the young woman insane. Sobbing, she waded out into the water and drowned as she frantically searched for her child.

Two real-life incidents are eerily similar. The first took place four years before San Francisco's devastating earthquake, and was covered in the following *San Francisco Call* June 26, 1902, issue.

Mother Rescues Child From Drowning

Adolph Pick, the five year old son of Morris Pick, a cigar packer residing at 4358 Clementine St. came near losing his life in Stow Lake in Golden Gate Park yesterday afternoon. The little fellow was playing along the edge of the lake when he lost his footing and fell into the water. His mother promptly plunged into the lake and rescued him. The ambulance was telephoned for and the mother and child were taken to the Park Emergency Hospital for treatment. Both were found to be none the worse for their bath.

Fifty years later another near drowning of a child was reported in the November 11, 1958, issue of the *Oakland Tribune*. The newspaper carried the story of a woman who had rescued her three-year-old from certain death when she pulled the drowning child from the lake. She was watching her older children play when the toddler wandered off.

But this isn't to say that death hasn't come to some at Stow Lake. The September 8, 1898, issue of the *San Francisco Call* reported that the body of a man had been found floating in the lake. Apparently, the man had been involved in a fight. He had a black eye, no identification, and save for a gold wedding ring (with the initials J. S. engraved inside), had nothing of value on his person. When no one came forward to claim the unknown man he was buried in a pauper's grave and forgotten.

Several years later, the victim was identified on January 30, 1906, as wealthy San Francisco miner John Stinson. Eager to see what fortune he had amassed, the family had his safe deposit box opened up. To everyone's surprise the box was empty. It now appeared that Stinson, who had mysteriously disappeared seven years earlier, had been killed for his money. Shortly before he vanished, he'd been in company of two men, and detectives appeared to be closing in on the killers in February.

On January 6, 1908, the *San Francisco Chronical* carried the front-page story of Arthur Pigeon, a man who claimed to have seen a ghost in Golden Gate Park. As the newspaper reported, Pigeon was escorting a car full of women from a party. Driving through Golden Gate Park, his mood and that of the ladies was one of carefree happiness—until a ghostly figure stepped out in the front of the car near Stow Lake.

Pigeon and his passengers were so frightened that he found the nearest police officer and reported the incident.

"The thing," he said, "was clad in a luminous white robe, and holding its arms extended as though to stop the progress of the machine. It was a thin tall figure. It appeared to shine. It had long fair hair and was barefoot."

When asked about the face, Pigeon replied, "I did not notice the face. I was too frightened."

Pigeon agreed to take the officer back to where he'd encountered the ghost. And as you might expect, there was no ghost in sight.

This first ghost sighting may be where the ghost story originated. According to legend, the way to summon the ghostly lady of Stow Lake is to utter the words, "White Lady, White Lady, I have your baby."

Say these words three times and the ghost will walk out of Stow Lake, dripping wet, and ask, "Have you seen my baby?"

Anyone answering "yes" will be haunted forever. But it gets worse. Anyone answering "no" will be killed by the ghostly lady.

When not in the water, the Stow Lake ghost is said to reside within the *Pioneer Mother* statue located near the lake's boathouse. The bronze statue was created in 1914 by Charles Grafly and was displayed at the Panama-Pacific International Exposition in 1915. The statue was moved to Golden Gate Park on December 18, 1940. At this writing it is the only statue of a woman within the park. It is also the only statue surrounded by strange phenomenon.

According to some, the sounds of children's disembodied laughter can be heard during the early morning, just as the sun is rising. After dark the statue comes to life, and occasionally turns its head from side to side, changes positions, and moves its arms as if beckoning someone. Even more horrifying is when the statue contorts its face in anger. A teenage couple that witnessed this fled the park swearing never to return.

Rodrigo's Haunted Adobe

*T*he Essanay Film Company discovered Niles Canyon in 1912 and made several of its western films here at the foot of the canyon. Charlie Chaplin's classic 1915 *The Tramp* was filmed here as well. Twenty years before Chaplin came to Niles Canyon, a reporter from the *San Francisco Call* met with the elderly Rodrigo Otero who lived near the canyon. It was October 18, 1896, Halloween was less than two weeks away and the reporter wanted information about the haunted adobe that was still standing.

Rodrigo was only too happy to oblige. The first thing he did was to warn the man never to go inside the deserted adobe. He knew about the dangers; his father had told him the stories when he was a boy. It was said that Satan himself had built the adobe, and over twenty men had met their deaths there in the past forty years. The Mexicans and Native Americans who lived nearby refused to go anywhere near the place.

They'd heard the bloodcurdling cries and seen the strange green lights late at night. Rodrigo told the writer of the skeletons and the ghosts his grandson had seen dancing in the adobe late at night. Too many men, including Rodrigo's father, had been murdered by Satan in and around the haunted adobe.

When pressed about an actual ghost, Rodrigo told the writer about seeing the ghost of his father. "My father, he was killed in there. But we never found the murderer. Of course not, it was the devil. But I have seen my father since, Señor, and he told me to keep away from the old house, he come out of his grave one night to tell me. Oh, but I was frightened. I was going to run, but he raised his hand and I stopped. I don't know what words he said, but I don't go near the house anymore."

"Keep away, Señor. Or we find you dead in the morning."

At the time of his interview, Rodrigo's haunted adobe was being used as a storehouse for the California Nursery Company founded by John Rock in San Jose in 1865 and relocated to Niles in 1884. The nursery's history dates to Jose de Jesus Vallejo (1797–1882), who was appointed administrator of the nearby Mission of San Jose in 1837. Five years later he received the grant of the Arroyo del Alameda rancho of over twenty thousand acres from Governor Alvarado. In 1853 Vallejo erected the flour mill on his property. In 1972 California Nursery Company grounds became a park known as the California Nursery Company Historical Park.

Within the twenty-acre park is the Vallejo Adobe built in 1842. According to the California Nursery Company website, the adobe was originally built as a bunkhouse and was later used for grain storage and for fumigation of trees. Today the adobe can be rented for parties and is most likely Rodrigo's haunted adobe.

Leland Stanford and Family

*T*he prestigious Stanford University was founded in 1885 by former California governor (1862–1863) and former state senator (1885–1893) Leland Stanford and his wife, Jane. Legend has it that they did so at the urging of the ghost of their only child, Leland Stanford Jr.

Shortly before winning the election, Stanford bought what is known as the Stanford Mansion for eight thousand dollars in 1861. He and Jane would have the mansion remodeled to suit their tastes, including having it raised twelve feet because of flooding of the nearby Sacramento River.

In the spring of 1884, the Stanford family was enjoying a tour of Europe when fifteen-year-old Leland Jr. fell ill. He died in Florence, two months shy of his sixteenth birthday. Leland Sr. and Jane were devastated. They'd doted on their son. Grief-stricken, they began looking at the afterlife in earnest. And in an effort to contact Leland Jr. they attended séances in Paris and in the US with popular medium of the day Maud Lord Drake. Although Leland Sr. and Jane would later deny it, Drake told the press that Stanford Jr. had come to them in a séance asking that his father build a university for the children of California. Leland Sr. called Drake a fraud and insisted the idea for the university had come to him in a dream.

The final resting place of the Stanford family—Leland Sr., Leland Jr., and Jane—is the Leland Family Mausoleum in the northwest corner of the Stanford University campus. On the last Friday or Saturday of October the sophomore class usually holds a Halloween Mausoleum Party there.

While sightings of Leland Sr. and Jr are occasionally reported, it's the ghostly Jane Stanford who's the most active. And she really gets around. Not only does she haunt the mausoleum and other areas of the university, Jane also makes appearances at the Stanford Mansion in downtown Sacramento and at the Moana Surfrider, a Westin

Resort & Spa, in Honolulu, Hawaii, where she died. She is a restless spirit indeed. And she has good reason to be so.

For all her money, all her good deeds, and all her celebrity, Mrs. Stanford died under mysterious circumstances on February 28, 1905. Mysterious in that she died of strychnine poisoning. And there is no logical explanation as to how the poison got into her bottle of bicarbonate of soda, or the identity of the person who put the poison in the bottle in the first place. It was all very hush-hush.

Stanford University wanted the Stanford money, but not the scandal of murder. So Jane Stanford was hastened to her grave before her time, and her murderer was permitted to walk free, not even a scintilla of scandal or suspicion clinging to his (or her) coattails.

No wonder those who've encountered her ghostly presence say she doesn't seem to be in the best of humor.

Al Jolson and Virginia Rappe at the Westin St. Francis

The ghostly man has been seen in Suites 1219 and 1221 on the twelfth floor of the Westin St. Francis many times since his untimely death here on October 23, 1950. He is Al Jolson who helped change the movie industry on October 6, 1927, with his role in the first sound movie *The Jazz Singer*. His famous line: "Wait a minute, wait a minute, I tell yer, you ain't heard nothin' yet."

Jolson was a big-time Broadway star. When sound came to film, he became an even bigger star. Naturally more offers and money poured in. During the Great Depression much of the country was thrown into poverty, but not Al Jolson. He was the country's highest paid entertainer. And for the next twenty-three years Al Jolson did what he loved; he traveled the world entertaining throngs of adoring fans.

Slated to appear on the Bing Crosby radio show, Jolson had come to San Francisco after entertaining Korean War troops. At the St. Francis he was playing rummy with friends when he grabbed his chest. "Call a doctor," he gasped.

When the doctor arrived at the suite Jolson explained that he was dying. While the doctor insisted this wasn't the case, Jolson touched his chest. "I'm going."

And sadly, he was right. Apparently, he hasn't gone that far. Al Jolson's ghost is still there on the twelfth floor, cards in hand. But he is not alone.

The weeping ghost of long-dead actress Virginia Rappe is also said to reside in suites 1219 and 1221. She occasionally walks the hallway of the twelfth floor in search of Roscoe "Fatty" Arbuckle, who was accused of raping her on September 9, 1921, thus causing her death. Arbuckle had come to San Francisco to party at the St. Francis during the Labor Day holiday. When Virginia Rappe and a friend showed up at his suite, they were welcomed and given drinks. The party ended abruptly two hours later with Virginia screaming in agonizing pain.

What had happened to her? Her friend claimed that Arbuckle raped her and was thus responsible for the starlet's death. The ensuing investigation, arrest, and trial would spell doom to Fatty Arbuckle's Hollywood career. The scandal haunted him for the rest of his life.

An interesting letter from Roy Jefferson, secretary of the International Psychical Research Society, appeared in the December 1921 issue of *Screenland* magazine. In the article titled "Is Virginia Rappe Alive?" Jefferson claimed that Virginia Rappe's ghost had materialized before an audience of 450 people during a society meeting.

> Shortly after the meeting started and during a violin solo, Virginia Rappe appeared as in a beautiful cloud. She gradually became a materialized form and was recognized by many. We were all astonished as she had not even been spoken of by anyone present. She was visible to all and said in a voice loud enough to be heard by many:
>
> "Roscoe Arbuckle is not guilty and I want justice done."
>
> She called a well-known press woman to her and said, "As a press woman you can help me and I want you to give this to the press so the world will know he is innocent."

On April 12, 1922, Roscoe Arbuckle was acquitted of manslaughter charges after three trials. His popularity was gone and his career was ruined. He died in New York City eleven years later.

As for the ghostly Virginia Rappe, she spends her time between the Westin St. Francis and the Hollywood Forever Cemetery in Los Angeles where she also is known to walk.

Sally Stanford Walks

In 1924 eighteen-year-old Mabel Janice Busby packed up and left Oregon forever. With her move to the City by the Bay she would become San Francisco's most successful madam. Her brothel on Nob Hill was known as the place where the world's movers and shakers came to be entertained by impeccably dressed, beautiful women. As she traveled the path to wealth, notoriety, and success in politics, fickle Sally was married and divorced five times.

It might have seemed perfectly fine to her clientele, but the law took a dim view of Sally's business. During her colorful career as a madam, she was arrested more than a dozen times, but only convicted twice. In the early 1940s Sally moved across the bay to the quaint little town of Sausalito and bought the Walhalla Biergarten on the boardwalk. She opened the restaurant as the Valhalla Inn. Film noir buffs may know that the Valhalla appears in the Orson Wells, Rita Hayworth classic *Lady from Shanghai.*

With Sally at the helm the restaurant prospered. It was not unusual to see a famous actor or actress sipping a drink at the bar or eating a meal in the dining room. Trouble came when Sally decided to brighten things up with a blazing neon sign. Sausalito city fathers were appalled at the ostentatious sign and quickly vetoed the idea. This is when Sally decided to run for office.

Her political career got off to a slow start. After six attempts and winning a seat on the Sausalito city council, Sally finally won in 1972. She wouldn't stop there. Sally would go on to become the mayor of Sausalito. And because of her colorful history, she was a regular guest on late night TV talk shows.

Sally died on February 1, 1982, at the age of seventy-nine. And her beloved Valhalla, like her Pine Street bordello, was razed to make way for progress. And yet—the ghostly Sally has been seen numerous times where Valhalla once stood. Her thick dark hair is elegantly coifed and she wears high fashion of the 1950s. She smiles and nods to anyone who happens to notice her, and then turns and slowly vanishes—just another friendly politician who happens to be a ghost. Then, too, there are the three ghostly women in 1940s attire who also wander the area. They are said to be women who might have worked in Sally's San Francisco bordello back in the day. Meanwhile Sally Stanford walks.

Winchester House

*T*he world-renowned Winchester House is without a doubt the most famous haunted house in California. At 24,000 square feet it is also the largest. With 160 rooms, 10,000 windows, 2,000 doors, 13 bathrooms, and 47 stairways and fireplaces how could it be otherwise?

Don't let those thirteen bathrooms fool you. When Sarah Winchester lived in the house only one was a working bathroom. The other twelve were merely decoys to confuse any unfriendly ghosts. And this is where the legend begins. According to a long-held story, Sarah Winchester lost her infant daughter and her husband in 1882, throwing her into deep depression. Hoping to contact her beloved William she attended a séance presented by Boston medium Adam Coons.

She was not just any widow. As the sole heir to the Winchester Rifle Company, Sarah was a very wealthy woman indeed. She was beside herself with grief and hoped that her husband might come to her through the medium with advice. Coons noticed the ghostly William Wirt Winchester standing near the heartbroken Sarah. But first, there were other more demanding spirits to contend with. They were victims of the Winchester rifle from which Sarah's inheritance stemmed. As atonement Sarah was told to go west and build a house in honor of those spirits.

She traveled to the Santa Clara Valley and purchased a six-room farmhouse and several hundred acres. She then hired craftsmen and carpenters to remodel and add on to the farmhouse using her specifications. But they were not entirely Sarah's. The spirits advised her to keep building. Legend has it that the superstitious Sarah believed she was cursed, but as long as carpenters were working on the house, she could not die. So work on the house proceeded 24/7.

To aid in her spirit communication, Sarah had a séance room built in the center of the house. She also had carpenters construct staircases that went nowhere and doors that opened onto nothing. And just to keep any ill-intentioned spirit away, she slept in a different bedroom every night. There is no question that Sarah Winchester was an eccentric woman who believed strongly in the afterlife. And according to many paranormal experts, she still roams the mansion. More than a century since her death people still come from around the world to experience a ghost at Sarah Winchester's house.

Sarah Winchester has been seen in the mansion countless times since her death at age eighty-three in 1922. Shortly after her death the house was opened for tours, and the paranormal activity began. Soon people were not only talking about the strange house, but the ghosts as well.

In 1924 famed magician and debunker of Spiritualism and fake paranormal claims, Harry Houdini came to see the house. While he enjoyed the séance room, he didn't encounter the ghostly Sarah, nor was he able to debunk any of the Winchester House's haunting claims. Others have come since then to explore and investigate the house, including the late Sylvia Brown, Zak Bagans, and the *Ghost Adventures* team. Their findings are a mixed bag of paranormal phenomena.

Visitors to the house report seeing ghostly servants and carpenters who have decided to spend eternity in the Winchester House. Some lucky people have seen Sarah Winchester herself in the hallway outside one of her bedrooms. Please don't try and talk to her. If you should, she's liable to give you a withering look and walk right into the nearest wall.

Tour guides have also encountered the supernatural at the Winchester House. Some tell of hearing ghostly footsteps in the hallways and of hearing their names called when they are alone. One of the most often spotted ghosts is a young man called Clyde. Clyde is busy at work either in the garden or in the basement. You'll know him because he's always pushing an antique wheelbarrow. A conscientious ghost who loves his work—just what you might expect at the most famous haunted house in California.

Tom Bowers's Ghost

Was Tom Bowers a real person or merely a composite that served as a warning to anyone who might consider claim jumping another man's claim stake? Regardless, the tale of Tom Bowers's ghost has been told since the days of the California gold rush.

Bowers, a man without friends or enemies, spent his days in the solitary pursuit of gold near Pike City. Bowers knew nothing about the men who worked nearby. And no one knew much about him. He liked it that way. It would be easier when he struck it rich. Bowers had no doubt that he would one day find gold—and become a wealthy man.

Before that day came, Tom Bowers fell over dead near the shaft of his mine. He'd kept to himself in life, but the other miners did the decent thing and buried Bowers. Within days there were strange noises that seemed to emanate from Bowers's mine. This frightened a few men away, but not everyone was afraid of things that go bump in the night.

Eventually another miner came to claim the abandoned mine. And in his quest for gold he worked just as diligently as Tom Bowers had. One night he was in the mine when a terrible noise seemed to arise from every corner. He grabbed his gun and waited. No one was going to scare him off with such tomfoolery.

Suddenly a glowing placard caught his eye. He moved closer to the placard and read the words, *Notice! I, Tom Bowers, claim this ground for placer mining.*

The hair on the back of the miner's neck rose up. Had Tom Bowers returned after all? He grabbed for the placard, only to see it vanish before his startled eye. The steady tap-tap-tap of a pick surrounded the mine. The frightened man's piercing screams could be heard as far away as the saloon.

Curious miners downed their drinks and ran to the mine shaft. No one was in sight. On the ground were a pick, a rifle, and a shovel with the initials T. B. carved into it. The mine was abandoned, and reasoning that there are some things more important than gold, no one ever again went near it.

Preston Castle

*G*host enthusiasts know it as Preston Castle, but it's no more a castle than your local grocery store is. This imposing, red-brick building in Ione was officially known as Preston School of Industry. When completed in 1890, it was to serve as a reform school, housing juvenile offenders and training them in skills they could use to better their lives.

The first of these offenders arrived in 1894. For the next sixty-six years hundreds of other juvenile offenders would be sent to Preston School of Industry. Some major talents in the fields of writing, acting, and music were incarcerated at Preston: Among them was actor Rory Calhoun and country western singer/songwriter Merle Haggard, who after a string of offenses was sent to San Quentin. In 1972 California governor Ronald Reagan granted a full and unconditional pardon to Merle Haggard for his crimes.

The 1978 film *Straight Time* starring Dustin Hoffman was based on the works of writer Edward Bunker who was an inmate of Preston, as was beat poet and writer Neal Cassady. Cassady is said to have greatly influenced Jack Kerouac's writing style. Those were the successes that went on to triumph in adversity. Caryl Chessman, the Redlight Bandit, didn't see the error of his ways, although he wrote several bestselling books while on death row and awaiting execution at San Quentin. Chessman was executed by the State of California on May 2, 1960.

Life at Preston School of Industry was hard. Punishment was severe. And violence was the norm.

The school closed in 1960 and was slated to be demolished. Luckily a group stepped in and halted the state's plans. Thus, the school would be mostly forgotten for the next several years—until the state gave the Preston Castle Foundation a lease, and eventually ownership of the building in 2014. The Preston Castle Foundation works tirelessly to preserve the old building and its history. This is done with the help of volunteers and members by offering tours and other events. Many of those events are ghost conferences.

Several years ago, Bill and I and our friend the late Robert Allen attended a paranormal conference presented by the late Doug Carnihan. Robert and I were speakers at the event and were eager to explore the old building during our off time. As we went from room to room, the one constant was the feeling of being watched. Thinking the logical explanation might be secret cameras, we looked in every place a lens could be hidden. We found nothing. Always quick with the joke, Robert said, "It's a wayward ghost tagging along with us."

Bill and I laughed. No sooner had we done so than an icy cold hand gently touched the back of my neck. It wasn't Bill. And it wasn't Robert, who stood across the room from us. Disconcerted and unable to get warm, I walked out of the building into the afternoon sunshine. It had been a gentle touch—and yet I knew there was something negative about it.

Right then and there I decided that as beautiful as this old building was, and as fascinating as its history was, I didn't like Preston Castle. And more importantly, Preston Castle didn't like me.

We got through our presentations in the basement with a silent thought of Anna Corbin, head housekeeper, whose body was discovered in a storeroom, beaten to death. The 1950 murder went unsolved, although some historians believe that an inmate by the name of Eugene Monroe was the killer. Anna is believed to be one of the ghostly residents of Preston Castle. She is, according to some mediums, a positive spirit unlike the negative one in residence.

We went to dinner, planning to return with the other conference attendees for a thrilling evening ghost investigation. There would be about forty of us and that would make for a decent investigation when we split up into groups. Our equipment was charged up; our hopes were high when we returned around ten that night. To our amazement the parking lot was full, and the place was teeming with ghost hunters. We couldn't figure out how forty had suddenly turned into more than a hundred. Perplexed, we asked questions. It seemed that tickets had been sold separately for the ghost investigation. And given Preston's popularity what did we expect?

Not this. We decided not to stay. There were just too many people for any kind of reliable investigation. So we said our goodbyes to Doug and a few others and headed back to Jackson and our hotel rooms. We would return to Preston Castle another time when it was less crowded.

When Bill and I returned next it was under very different circumstances—a private investigation. During my first EVP session I asked if whoever had touched my neck was present. No response.

"Why did you touch my neck?"

I received no answers to the question. However, I did record the following.

"Do you like it here at Preston?" I asked

"I want out!" a voice answered.

"Were you an inmate here?" I asked.

"I am all alone."

I left knowing that my first assessment had been correct. I didn't like Preston Castle. And Preston Castle didn't like me.

Lyle's Room

*S*ituated in California's Gold Country, the town of Groveland boomed during the California gold rush that began in 1848. By 1855 the gold had dwindled and the gold rush was over. Many of the miners moved on. A few of them stayed and settled into other jobs in the area. Groveland may have become a ghost town if not for the Hetch Hetchy water project that was created to bring drinking water to the San Francisco area.

The controversial Hetch Hetchy spanned twenty-five years from 1913 to 1938 and in that time Groveland once again boomed. The little town that is located on the highway to Yosemite National Park welcomed nearly ten thousand new residents. There were at least seven hotels in Groveland. The oldest was the Groveland Hotel that was built in 1859. The quaint, old hotel is still in operation today. And if you happen to choose to stay in Room 115, you'll be sleeping in the ghostly Lyle's room.

Lyle is believed to be the ghost of an old miner who was at the Groveland Hotel and sleeping peacefully, with a box of dynamite under his bed, when the grim reaper came calling for him. There's no reason for him to vacate the premises. The hotel keeps the room as close to how it was in Lyle's day with a few modern conveniences, of course. The ghostly Lyle doesn't bother anyone, but he is persnickety. Ladies, do not leave your cosmetics strewn across *his* dresser. He won't like it and has been known to shove all such beauty paraphernalia to the floor. When the mood strikes, usually in the wee hours of the morning, Lyle likes to turn the water faucets on and off, on and off. Likewise, the lights; no it's not a power surge. It's only Lyle having some fun.

If you've chosen to stay in Lyle's room, you obviously enjoy the thrill of spending some time with a ghost and his unpredictable antics. Just remember neatness is the order of the day. Don't leave your cosmetics in your case and don't scatter papers or candy wrappers about. Now plump up the pillows and get set for a good night's sleep—or not.

Central California

Monterey Hotel

*W*ith breathtaking scenic beauty, and a colorful cultural history that dates to before the founding of the United States, the Monterey Peninsula is a richly haunted place. Each year approximately eight million visitors come here. Whether they come for business or pleasure, it's not unusual for a tourist to have an occasional ghostly encounter, especially in Monterey, one of California's oldest cities. And here I'll say that there is a misconception on the East Coast that the West Coast's history is somewhat newer than that of the East.

In 1770, six years before the Declaration of Independence was signed, the city of Monterey was established by Father Junipero Serra and Gaspar de Portola. Monterey served as California's capital from 1777 to 1849, first under the rule of Spain and then Mexico. In 1850 California became the thirty-first state, with Monterey serving briefly as its capital.

California had been a state for nearly sixty years when the Monterey Hotel opened its doors on Alvarado Street on March 16, 1904. The ghostly resident here is known as Fred, a former employee who died on the premises several years ago. And while the ghostly Fred takes special delight in his little pranks, he is not a malicious ghost. However, he does favor women. Curious, my husband and I spent a weekend at the elegant hotel in the heart of downtown recently.

When we explained our intentions to learn more about Fred to staff, none were shy about sharing their experiences with the ghostly resident. One employee eagerly told of a man who came to stay two nights at the hotel. He angrily cut his stay short because he insisted that a ghost was playing with his television. Did I say that Fred was the maintenance man who was in charge of keeping room TVs in working order? Another longtime employee we'll call Amy said, "Fred has always been nice to me. But he didn't like the night auditor. He trapped the man in his office one night even though the door was wide open. No matter how many times he tried to walk out that door, Fred blocked his way and wouldn't let him pass."

Amy shook her head and smiled. "Eventually he let the man out, of course. But that was enough. The man gave notice soon after that."

When asked what else the prank-playing Fred does, Amy replied, "He sometimes turns the telephones off or causes them to ring. But now that everyone has a cellphone he seems to have lost interest. He still messes with the televisions . . . he really likes to play with them. Guests will complain that their sets aren't working, but when someone goes up to check they are working just fine."

She told us that Fred prefers the basement and agreed to accompany us down the stairs for an impromptu EVP session. With two digital recorders running, we descended into the basement, calling for Fred to join us. We spent several minutes asking questions and taking photos. On this night it appeared that Fred was uncommunicative. It was getting late, we were tired, and she had to get back upstairs. We thanked Fred and ended our session by asking him if he had a message for Amy who was in the basement with us.

Weeks later, we were home and I was listening to the recordings. All our questions were met with silence, except for one. When I asked, "Fred do you have a message for Amy?", very clearly someone whispered, "Stop it."

We may never know whether Fred was telling us to stop asking questions or telling Amy that he wanted something stopped.

Cannery Row's Ghosts

*T*he Cannery Row of today is nothing like that described in Pulitzer- and Nobel Prize–winning writer John Steinbeck's bestselling books *Cannery Row* and *Sweet Thursday*. Today's row is a place of upscale hotels, restaurants, and shops. Once known as Ocean Avenue, the street was renamed in 1958 in honor of Steinbeck's 1945 *Cannery Row*. Where laborers once toiled long, grueling hours in fish packing facilities are now the Monterey Bay Aquarium, eateries, and shops carved from the skeletons of those old buildings. The ghosts of the men and women who lived and died here still walk Cannery Row.

One of them is said to be Knut Hovden, owner of the Hovden Canning Company, present-day site of the Monterey Bay Aquarium. The innovative Hovden, once known as King of Cannery Row, was a workaholic who loved his work. A man of vision, Knut Hovden suggested an aquarium be created for the Row in the 1920s.

Hovden died in 1961, two decades before the aquarium became a reality—a reality born of the old building that once was Hovden's. And this may be why the ghostly Hovden has been spotted in the aquarium on more than one occasion. Those who've seen him say he seems curious as he intensely *inspects* the Hovden Canning exhibit.

The ghosts of the men and women who worked in the canneries are also occasionally seen milling around the spots where once they spent long hours packing fish into tins, head to tail, head to tail.

My mother and my grandmother both worked in the canneries. I remember how tired they were when they returned home each night. And although they wore heavy aprons, the strong odor of fish emanated from their clothing. My mother still talks of the supervisors who were difficult and harsh to work with.

The laboratory of John Steinbeck's close friend Ed Ricketts (immortalized as Doc in *Cannery Row* and *Sweet Thursday*) is located at 800 Cannery Row. Open to the public on occasion, the lab is where the *ghostly* Ricketts is said to unobtrusively watch visitors. A recent visitor to the lab explained, "He wasn't concerned with me. But he sure seemed interested in how things were set up."

More than one visitor has had the chilling experience of brushing up against the ghostly Ed Ricketts as he makes his way around his beloved old laboratory. This is especially so if the visitor happens to be female. The marine biologist didn't spend all his time exploring the rugged Monterey coast and writing scholarly books. He was also known as a ladies' man.

Sightings of Ed Ricketts most often occur at dusk near the bust located at Wave Street and Drake Avenue that commemorates him. The bust was placed at the spot where he was fatally injured on May 8, 1948, when the *Del Monte Express* crashed into his car on the railroad tracks. The tracks have long since been removed and given way to a bike trail, but the ghostly Ed Ricketts doesn't seem to realize this.

While Ricketts has been seen day and night on Cannery Row, his dear friend John Steinbeck prefers to wander the Row late at night in reminiscence of how things once were. The ghostly habitué of the Row who draws a lot more male attention is a pretty young woman. It's believed that she plied her trade at Flora Adams's Lone Star Brothel back in the day. The friendly miss is said to stop and plant a kiss on men who happen to be walking the Row alone late at night. One stunned man watched as she fled toward Flora's place.

Malpaso

*N*o one is really sure who she is, but some believe the ghostly lady in white who's been seen in and around the Mission San Juan Bautista plaza is Encarnacion Sanchez Godden Sanford Crane Alviso. Those who've encountered the lady say she seems to be unhappy and is crying. Encarnacion led a difficult life. A beautiful woman, Encarnacion was married five times. According to one legend, her husbands all fell victim to what was known as the Curse of the Sanchez Treasure.

Thus, the ghostly woman, whose life was thrown into tumult by a curse, walks the plaza, keeping her secrets and nodding sadly if anyone should notice her.

Don Jose Maria Sanchez came to California from Mexico as a young man in 1825. He formed a partnership with Francisco Perez Pacheco who had been granted over thirty-five thousand acres by a Mexican land grant. The partnership prospered with the two men becoming very wealthy. In 1840 Sanchez married Encarnacion Ortega, a beautiful woman twenty years his junior. The marriage produced four children, but Sanchez was a heavy gambler and Encarnacion didn't like the way he lost their money; neither spouse was happy in the marriage.

On Christmas Eve 1852 Sanchez was headed home from a very profitable business trip, or a winning card game (depending on which story you believe), in the high Sierra. His heavy canvas bags were laden with gold coins. He may have thought of his wife and how she would be thrilled with the gold; he would be more generous with her. He might even permit her to buy herself and the children some of the baubles and trinkets she so craved. Yes, there would be many celebrations tomorrow.

According to some legends, Don Jose Maria Sanchez had stopped along the trail earlier and buried half of his gold coins in a spot known only to himself. Whether he did this or not matters little to the outcome of our story. So we'll continue on the lonely ride with Señor Sanchez.

As he neared his beloved Rancho Lomerias Muertas, Sanchez encountered torrential rains that pounded the earth, causing the swollen San Benito and Pajaro Rivers to flood their banks and spread out across the valley. Angry winds swept through the region uprooting trees and tearing houses and barns apart.

Exhausted and soaked to the bone by his long, cold ride in the downpour, Jose Maria Sanchez urged his horse onward. His family was waiting. Horse and rider came to the soggy banks of the Pajaro River at Malpaso Creek. Sensing danger, the horse balked. Don Sanchez squinted; even in the darkness, he could see the river roiling like never before. He stroked the horse's crest and spoke gently.

"Lo siento mi amigo. There is no other way to get across. We must do this."

As if in agreement, the animal started into the raging river. But the river's bottom was soft as quicksand, and just as deadly. The horse lost its footing; Don Sanchez was thrown into the icy waters. Thus separated, horse and rider were quickly swept away from one another.

When daybreak came with still no sign of her husband, wifely apprehension gnawed at Encarnacion. This was Christmas Day; absence on such a holy day was not like him at all. By mid-morning the rain finally let up and servants set out in the cold fog to locate the lost Don Sanchez. The Pajaro had receded revealing bodies of lost animals and people. Don Sanchez was not among them. Perhaps, some speculated, his body had washed far out into the Pacific Ocean.

As the day wore on sunshine shoved through dense patches of fog; if it was a sign of better days to come, no one in the fine adobe house noticed. Christmas was forgotten as a terrible pall fell over the Rancho Lomerias Muertas. Encarnacion quietly walked the floors and wept. She was saddened, not for herself, but for her children. Not only had their father met a terrible fate, but his body was lost to them forever and there could not be a burial in the San Juan Cemetery. She had no husband, but this did not cause her heart to ache;

she had long ago fallen out of love with the ruthless, cruel man her husband had become in their twelve years of marriage. As the beautiful widow of a wealthy man, she would survive.

Alone in San Juan, Encarnacion knew there were whispers of Sanchez and the riches he had left her, and of the gold that was hidden somewhere on the other side of the Pajaro. She must not allow any grass to grow under her feet. She must make haste lest some unscrupulous person wrest her late husband's fortune from her and the children.

In a time when what women wanted mattered less than the dust on a prospector's boots, the young widow found herself facing formidable men whose palms itched in greedy anticipation of the Sanchez fortune. Rumors spread through Monterey faster than wildfire across the parched dry hills of Arroyo Seco; people talked of little else but the thousands of dollars in gold coins the Don was said to have buried somewhere on his Rancho Lomerias Muertas. Lucky indeed would be the man who could find and claim this cache.

On January 5, 1853, Encarnacion took her place in the second-floor courtroom of Colton Hall. Judge Josiah Merritt cast a steely eye on the group that had assembled to hear the Sanchez probate case. One Antonio Chavez stepped forward and told the court he had witnessed the unfortunate drowning of Don Jose Maria Sanchez in the raging Pajaro. He had nothing in the way of evidence to prove his assertions, but his words were enough. Don Sanchez was dead and his estate needed to be probated. Without consulting the widow, Merritt appointed a young farmer by the name of Jesse Smith to act as administrator of the Sanchez estate. Smith turned and smiled at Encarnacion, greed glinting in his eyes.

She went back to San Juan a frightened woman; the gold rush had brought Americans to California in search of great riches. When the gold dried up they turned to the fertile land. No matter that the Mexicans owned it legally; the Americans took the land and called it theirs. Would it be the same with the Sanchez land? She could not fight them all. As it turned out, she wouldn't have to.

Young and handsome attorney Thomas P. Godden was newly arrived in San Juan. When he heard of the young widow's plight, he was willing to help her in her claim to her husband's money. As a

Spanish translator, Godden would be able to explain the intricacies of English to Encarnacion, who understood little of the American's language. But as the weeks wore on, Encarnacion became interested in Godden for reasons of a more romantic nature. His virility had not escaped her notice. And just as she was impressed with his good looks, he was likewise enchanted with her wealth and her beauty.

Two months after the tragic death of her first husband, Encarnacion married Thomas P. Godden. For the first time in many years she was truly happy. Her happiness would be short-lived, as bad luck, or *malpaso*, continued to follow her.

Smoke no longer spiraled day and night from the rancho's squat adobe chimney. The frosty days of winter faded into memory as spring came, turning the nearby hills green. Business beckoned Thomas Godden.

"I must take a short trip to San Francisco, my dearest," he announced over dinner on the eve of his parting. "I've important business that I must attend to. But you need not worry yourself over it. I shall travel alone to the city, and return before you even notice that I am gone."

Encarnacion doubted that. She missed Thomas whenever he was out of her sight more than a few minutes. And on the morning of his departure, she clung to her groom of two months and kissed him tenderly, never guessing it would be the last time she ever set eyes on him. An explosion on board the steamship *Jenny Lind* took the lives of several passengers; Godden was among the dead. And once again Encarnacion was a widow with another estate to probate.

Grief-stricken as she was at the loss of Thomas, she noticed that the superstitious servants shrank in fear, lest her bad luck somehow attach itself whenever she neared them. So be it; she still had to preserve the Sanchez fortune for its rightful owners, the Sanchez children. The task was daunting; she could not do it alone. No, she would need the help of an American man who understood how the greedy American mind worked. So she turned to Dr. Henry Sanford, an acquaintance of several years standing.

He was very kind, but not as handsome as Thomas Godden and certainly not as wealthy as Jose Maria. Nonetheless, she allowed herself to fall in love with him. Two months after the death of Thomas

Godden, Encarnacion married husband number three. Would the curse of Malpaso be broken? Two years passed. Perhaps the fates had conspired to see that she enjoyed not the giddy romance of youth, or the heady passion she and Thomas had known, but the more comfortable life she and Henry shared. Just when she convinced herself that it was so, another spring morning came bringing widowhood and a third estate to probate. In trying to help her recover money that rightfully belonged to her and her children, Henry Sanford had been shot and killed.

While the Sanchez case slowly worked its way through probate, Encarnacion and her children continued to be swindled out of their estate by unscrupulous businessmen and lawyers. When a young attorney by the name of George Crane came forward and promised to help her, Encarnacion grabbed the lifeline that he offered. And as it seemed to happen in her affairs of the heart, Encarnacion became Crane's wife within two months of making his acquaintance.

But there was a prenup to end all prenups. While Crane promised his faithfulness and loyalty and sealed the deal with a five-dollar gold piece, Encarnacion was more generous; she signed over the entire Sanchez estate to her new spouse. Twelve years passed. The Cranes' marriage was long and happy; Malpaso was defeated. Winter came to San Juan; bone-chilling fog swept in on the icy ocean breezes and clung to the hills day and night. Illness crept through town claiming the lives of anyone too old or too weak to fight off its effects.

On November 2, 1868, a cold chill set George Crane's teeth chattering. Wrapped in a woolen blanket, he pulled his chair closer to the fire. A raging fever surged through his body, yet he shivered. Encarnacion knew the symptoms; she'd heard of others who suffered in the same way. Fear clamped down on her. Even as she persuaded her husband to return to his bed, she realized there was no hope. She stroked his forehead and spoke softly to him. He was dead before the sun slid behind the hills.

Encarnacion was still lovely at forty-four years old; dare she take another mate? What was left of the Sanchez estate had long been settled, her children were grown, and loneliness closed in on her. At forty-seven, she married her fifth husband, Anastacio Alviso. One fall morning shortly after the marriage, Alviso set out on a hunting trip. Malpaso rode with him; during the hunt, an inexperienced hunter sited his prey and raised his rifle. Taking careful aim, he pulled the trigger; the bullet struck Anastacio Alviso in the heart, killing him instantly.

Encarnacion would live another twenty years, but she wisely chose to never again marry.

She is buried at the San Juan Bautista Cemetery. And on restless nights when the scent of the ocean is carried on the wind as it whips through tall eucalyptus trees, she keeps a lonely vigil in the plaza near the old mission.

Mission San Juan Bautista

It's said that every one of California's twenty-one missions is haunted. Mission San Juan Bautista is no exception. Founded by Father Fermín Francisco de Lasuén on June 24, 1797, San Juan Bautista is the fifteenth and the largest mission. It is also the only mission in the state with an original Spanish plaza.

Classic film buffs may remember that Mission San Juan Bautista is seen in Alfred Hitchcock's 1958 thriller, *Vertigo*. Another, not so fun fact is that the mission was built upon the San Andreas Fault, the fault line that extends eight hundred miles along coastal California. San Andreas is the most dangerous fault line, and is responsible for San Francisco's devastating 1906 earthquake, as well as California's other major earthquakes.

It was during a mild earthquake that we heard the footsteps of the ghostly padre. We were admiring a window when we realized a mild earthquake was rattling the old mission. It was over in an instant and all was quiet once more. All quiet except for footsteps coming toward us at a rapid pace. I turned to see who was in such a hurry. My husband and I were alone on the walkway.

Legend has it that a ghostly padre, his feet slapping on the tile walkways, can sometimes be heard in the early morning hours as he goes about his daily chores. It may be this same padre that's been seen in the mission's Indian cemetery on the north side of the church, where nearly four thousand Spanish and Mexican settlers, Mutsun, Yokut, and Miwok (Native Americans who helped build the mission) are buried. He chats briefly with a man who tends the graves, and then both vanish as quickly as they appeared.

Ghost hunters visiting the area have told of hearing Gregorian chants softly emanating from the mission in the predawn hours when no one is about. This well could be Father Pedro Estevan Tápis and his ghostly choir as they go about their practice. Father Tápis came to the mission in 1815 to teach Native Americans music. He created the mission's Native American choir; by using four-color coding, he made it possible for the singers to know what part was theirs. He was so successful in his endeavors that the Mission San Juan Bautista became known as the Mission of Music. Perhaps the music continues on.

Pacheco Pass

*E*very state has its dangerous roadways. Pacheco Pass on Highway 152 separates Los Banos in the Central Valley and Gilroy in the Santa Clara Valley, and is one of California's most notorious. In the last decades, scores of people have been killed in horrific head-on collisions here, particularly after dark, making Pacheco Pass the roadway with the most fatalities in the state. With its sordid history, many people won't drive Pacheco Pass, day or night.

Located in the Diablo Range, Pacheco Pass was named after Don Francisco Perez Pacheco whose large land grant from Mexico included the land upon which the pass sits. Belying its deadly history, the scenic drive passes the manmade San Luis Reservoir and the Pacheco State Park.

In the late 1800s this route was known as Robber's Pass for the two criminals who preyed upon travelers along the route. Pacheco Pass is said to be cursed by the bloody skirmishes that took place here between settlers and Native Americans. There is also the time warp. Motorists along this stretch of highway claim to have been transported to another time and witnesses to stagecoaches racing across the land. Some also report feelings of great unhappiness, distress, and foreboding as their vehicle makes its way across Pacheco Pass. Travelers at night have reported seeing strange lights in the sky over San Luis Reservoir. And then there are the ghosts.

A lone motorist was listening to his radio and trying to stay awake when he suddenly realized he was no longer alone in his vehicle. A glowing man in western attire sat in the passenger seat, staring straight ahead as the car made its way west. Testing to see if he was dreaming or not, the motorist reached to turn the radio off. As he did so he focused on the passenger seat. His ghostly passenger seemed oblivious to him. When the car crested the hill near Dinosaur Point, his passenger vanished. Wide awake now, the man had no trouble staying awake for the rest of his journey. The sudden appearance of a ghostly passenger seems to be a common occurrence along Pacheco Pass.

A woman and two small children in clothing of the late 1800s are occasionally spotted in the distance on the side of the road. They are believed to be the victims of long-ago killers. Those who've seen them say they seem to glimmer and dissolve as a car passes nearby. Perhaps the ghostly trio serves as sentinels warning motorists to be careful as they drive Pacheco Pass.

The Hitchhiking Ghost of Mount Madonna

Santa Clara County's 4,605-acre Mount Madonna Park is ten miles west of Gilroy, the Garlic Capital of the World. With redwood forests, meadows, and views of Monterey Bay, Mount Madonna Park offers overnight camping sites, horseback riding, and walking trails. It's plain to see why the park is a favorite with outdoor enthusiasts.

Between the late nineteenth century and early twentieth century, cattle baron Henry Miller was known as the Cattle King of California, and one of the country's largest landowners with 1.4 million acres in California, Nevada, and Oregon. The land comprising modern day Mount Madonna Park was included in Miller's vast landholdings. It was here near the summit of Mount Madonna peak that the Miller summer home was located. And it's here that our ghost story begins.

At eight Sarah Alice was the Millers' youngest child. Henry Miller doted on the little girl he called Gussie, seeing her as the closest to him in temperament. In her brief life, Sarah became a good horse rider, enjoying long rides. Tragedy struck on the morning of June 14, 1875, when Sarah Miller's horse stepped into a hole and tumbled to the ground. Sarah was thrown from the horse, breaking her neck in the fall. The grief-stricken Millers buried their beloved Sarah at Mount Madonna.

Twenty-five years after Sarah's untimely death, Miller helped found the town of Gustine in Central California, which was named after her nickname, Gussie. Although he would live another forty-one years, Henry Miller never completely recovered from the loss. When he died in 1916 Sarah Miller was exhumed and buried beside him in Colma. Ghost researchers believe that grief can cause a ghost to remain earthbound. Perhaps this is why little Sarah Miller has chosen to stay at Mount Madonna all these years.

A ghostly glowing horse and rider have been seen throughout the area where Sarah took her ill-fated ride on that long-ago morning. There have also been reports of the anguished cries of a little girl in the area calling out for help. Would-be rescuers spend hours searching for the girl only to discover that she is a ghost. Another more disconcerting sighting of the ghostly Sarah has been seen by drivers late at night on the road to Mount Madonna.

Imagine it's a rainy night and you are all alone in your car. Your windshield wipers slap out a somber tune reminding you that you have miles to go before you reach your destination. You happen to glance in the rearview mirror only to see a ghostly little girl staring back at you from the backseat. This has happened to more than one driver over the years. But not to worry, she vanishes almost as quickly as she appears. Sarah has also been spotted on the side of the road—waiting for a ride. Many people stop. It's then that they realize the little girl is merely a visitor from the hereafter.

Point Pinos Lighthouse

In operation since February 1, 1855, Point Pinos Lighthouse in Pacific Grove is the oldest continuously operating lighthouse on the West Coast. The first lighthouse keeper at Point Pinos was Charles Layton. Sadly, he would not hold the job for very long.

Feeling it his civic duty, Layton joined the posse that was purposed with bringing notorious California bandit Anastacio Garcia to justice. This decision ended badly for both Layton and Garcia. When the posse cornered him outside of Salinas, Garcia pulled his pistol and fired wildly, striking Layton in the stomach. Layton died a short time later from the wound, leaving behind a wife and four children. Garcia was taken to a Monterey jail where he was hanged the following year. City leaders agreed to give Charlotte Layton her husband's job as lighthouse keeper in order to finish out his term.

Thus, Charlotte was the first woman to have watched over the lighthouse. She was lighthouse keeper for four years, until she fell in love with her assistant and married him.

The next woman to be appointed lighthouse keeper at Point Pinos was Emily Fish in 1893. The fifty-year-old widow would hold the position for twenty-one years. In a time when women didn't enjoy the same rights as men, that was remarkable. But then, so was Emily Maitland Fish. After having her stylish furnishings moved in, Mrs. Fish's first act as lighthouse keeper was to remodel its living quarters. Clearly, Emily Fish did not fit the description as a lonely, introverted lighthouse keeper. She enjoyed entertaining friends at the lighthouse and was known as the socialite keeper for her parties and soirees.

Unlike other lighthouses, Point Pinos was not isolated. It was easily accessible and included ninety-four acres of land upon which Mrs. Fish raised horses and chickens and planted trees and shrubs. She insisted that everything inside and out always be tidy and in order.

She died in 1931 far from her beloved Point Pinos. But time and distance haven't kept her from the lighthouse. The ghostly Mrs. Fish is blamed for things that are moved from one location to another. The sound of her long skirt swishing through the building has also been reported. The following comes from a woman who visited the lighthouse in the 1970s as a child.

> I was about eleven and my grandmother was visiting from Seattle. We went to Asilomar and then to Point Pinos. My mom and grandmother were in the next room admiring the view. I was curious about a tool that was sitting on a table. I reached out to touch it. This is when I felt a sharp whack on my hand like someone had slapped it. There was no one in that room but me. I don't know who or what it was. Yet, I know it happened.

I'm guessing it was Mrs. Fish wanting nothing disturbed and moved out of order. But it could just as easily have been the unfortunate Mr. Layton, who is also said to be residing at Point Pinos. Layton prefers the solace of the upstairs area and rarely ventures elsewhere.

Several years ago during one of our visits to the peninsula, my husband, Bill, and I visited Point Pinos with our brand-new Sony Mavica digital camera. Digital cameras were just coming onto the market and we couldn't wait to put ours into action. First on our agenda was the lighthouse. As we stood on a layer of dry pine needles underneath tall pine trees, we discussed how many floppy discs we had and what angle would produce the best shot.

Suddenly a man was standing beside us. We were both stunned because neither of us had heard him approach. He smiled broadly. "What sort of camera is that?" he asked. "We don't have cameras like that."

We proudly explained the camera. As the conversation went on, we told him that we were at the lighthouse in hopes of getting a photo of the ghostly resident. "Ghosts," he chuckled. "If you want a real haunted lighthouse you need to go to Point Sur. They give ghost tours on full moon nights and tonight's a full moon. Go on inside and tell them the docent sent you to get a brochure about Point Sur."

We thanked him and he turned and headed toward a large group of people. Bill went inside to ask about Point Sur's ghost tour while I continued taking photos by the pine trees. For some reason, I stopped and watched as the man neared the people. He did not acknowledge them and they did not acknowledge him. *Odd for such an affable docent,* I thought. Imagine my surprise when Bill returned to tell me that the woman in the lighthouse had informed him that they had no docents on the grounds that day. We looked in the direction the man had headed. And he was nowhere in sight. By that time the fog was starting to roll in. We looked across the street at El Carmelo Cemetery.

Do you suppose . . .

No. Neither of us wanted to think about it.

The Ghost Bride of Pescadaro Point

*P*ebble Beach offers some of the most spectacular scenery in the world. It also offers some of the highest priced real estate in the US. But it is the tale of the ghost bride that brings ghost hunters to Pescadaro Point at Pebble Beach. This lady in tattered white lace is usually spotted on fog-shrouded nights walking down Seventeen Mile Drive toward the Monterey cypress trees that only grow naturally here at Pebble Beach and at Point Lobos. She stops and weeps at the gnarled tree known as the ghost tree.

As might be expected, there are a few legends that answer the question, who is the ghost bride?

One legend has it that the beautiful young woman was jilted by her lover at the church altar. With Montereyans whispering behind their fans, the humiliation was too much for her to bear. Crying hysterically, she set out toward the ghost tree ready to leap to her death. She was saved from her suicidal jump when she was hit and killed by a horse and buggy racing its way through the foggy night. Now she wanders the road for all eternity, aimlessly looking for her errant fiancée.

Others say she is not a bride at all, but rather, Dona Maria del Carmen Barreto, a wealthy woman who owned all the land that encompasses Seventeen Mile Drive; indeed, all of Pebble Beach. A reckless young woman, without the guidance of those older and wiser, she sold the land and lived to regret it. She returns on foggy nights to keep watch over what once belonged to her.

And yet another legend has her as a young, wealthy woman who lost the land because of her bad financial decisions and gambling losses. Regretting her foolishness, she dressed in her most elegant lace dress, walked out to Pescadaro Point, and leapt into the water far below. On foggy nights, she retraces her route, possibly hoping for a better outcome to her dilemma.

Whoever she was, the ghost bride of Pescadaro Point has been sought by ghost hunters for some time. While skeptics insist the ghost is nothing more than light reflecting in the fog, the ghost bride continues walking her lonely path.

The Dark Watchers

The Santa Lucia Mountain Range extends 140 miles down the California coastline from Carmel to San Luis Obispo. Located in the Santa Lucias is Cone Peak at 5,158 feet, the highest and nearest peak to the ocean in the contiguous United States. But there is another equally interesting fact about the Santa Lucias. And that is the mysterious Dark Watchers who live within the Santa Lucia Mountains near Big Sur.

The Dark Watchers have been called shadow people, ghosts, and even mysterious beings from another planet. No one is quite sure who they are or where they come from. People have been telling stories of the Dark Watchers for generations. Early Spanish settlers referred to them as Los Vigilantes Oscuros (Dark Watchmen).

They are reportedly seen at dusk or twilight, these giant entities that stand anywhere from seven to fifteen feet tall. Their heads are covered in wide brim black hats and their long black cloaks billow in the wind as they stare at something the living cannot see.

While they seem to be aware of the activity around them, the Dark Watchers apparently wish to have no contact with the living. If anyone should get too close to these dark entities, they vanish into thin air. Such was the case of a man who was hiking in the Santa Lucias with a friend. When he noticed a dark figure staring intently, he called out to his friend, "You've got to see this."

The entity vanished before he finished his sentence. Who are they and what do they want? No one has the answer to that question.

At least two mid-twentieth-century California writers were fascinated with the Dark Watchers. John Steinbeck wrote of the watchers in his 1938 short story "Flight," and in 1937 renowned Carmel poet Robison Jeffers wrote of them in his poem "Such Counsels You Gave to Me."

Debbie and the Ghostly Pirate

*M*y friend Debbie Hollingsworth, who happens to be a psychic medium, was visiting us one summer when we decided to introduce her to Monterey. Debbie and I'd shared many ghost hunting adventures, so Bill and I felt she would be amazed with the ghostly aspects of the Monterey Peninsula. We had no idea how amazed she would be.

After visiting the usual tourist sights, we drove out to Point Lobos, a favorite of ours. We visited the whaler's cabin and various trails and ended up on Bird Rock Trail. Debbie stopped to contemplate the view while Bill and I, anxious to get to China Cove, turned and walked in the opposite direction. When after a few minutes she hadn't joined us, we turned back to see where she was. She was still staring out at Bird Rock.

"Debbie," I called out.

She turned and motioned us toward her. "What's up?" I asked as we approached.

"Did you see him?" she asked.

"Who?" Bill and I asked in unison.

"The pirate," she said. "He was dressed like Johnny Depp as Captain Jack Sparrow. He just appeared there." She pointed to a spot near the trail's edge. "He was very handsome and he said, "Come back to me. Come back to me and we can be together forever. I could feel him touching me—and I could have easily stepped into his arms and been gone forever."

"He wanted you to jump into the water?" I asked gazing down at the water.

"No, he wanted me to go with him. I wonder if anyone's ever jumped or fallen here before," she said.

"No, but there's been a lot of shipwrecks here," Bill informed her. "Maybe your pirate was on one of those that sank to the bottom of the ocean."

"Maybe," she shuddered. "He was so real. And he made me feel that I should be with him—"

I laughed. "I'm glad you didn't go with him."

"Me too," she chuckled. "He was a male siren. And I've got to be honest with you; there was one split second when I thought about chucking it all and going with him."

Later we discovered that sirens of Greek mythology were bird women. And this had occurred on Bird Rock Trail with Bird Rock in sight. The ghostly pirate, we agreed, sure knew how to mix his metaphors.

Steinbeck House

> The house in Salinas is pretty haunted now. I see
> things walking at night that it is not good to see.
> —John Steinbeck writing to a friend
> about his boyhood home

It's ironic that someone who was purported to be a disbeliever in all things ghostly is haunting the house where he was born and raised. According to some, this is exactly what John Steinbeck is doing. With his bestselling works *Cannery Row, Tortilla Flat,* and *East of Eden,* writer Steinbeck brought worldwide attention to the Monterey Peninsula. His fans still come to see and experience the locations he wrote about.

The truly devoted will stop at Steinbeck's birthplace and boyhood home, a Victorian house located at 132 Central Avenue in Salinas. The Valley Guild, a nonprofit volunteer organization, runs the Steinbeck House, which offers an array of meals that feature local Salinas Valley produce, wines, and beer.

While waiting for their meals, patrons are free to look in the front bedroom where John Steinbeck was born, and gaze at family photo albums and other memorabilia. While doing so, someone will occasionally catch a glimpse of a ghostly woman standing on the stairs. Her identity is a mystery. No one, other than guild members, is permitted upstairs where Steinbeck and his sister skated as youngsters on rainy days, and where he later penned the classic *Red Pony.*

Also on the premises is the Best Cellar, a gift shop that features Steinbeck books, recipes from the restaurant (yummy), and assorted gifts. What do you suppose John, as the guild members refer to him, would have thought of all this attention? All these people paying homage to him by partaking of an afternoon repast in his old home might have seemed humorous to him. Is that why John Steinbeck himself is said to haunt the premises?

Diners often witness a ghostly man that fits the writer's description. But there were also reports of an elderly man's face being seen in the windows years before Steinbeck died. Those who saw him said the man seemed forlorn and his face was glowing red. Who he was or what he wanted was never determined.

There is one tale that claims John Steinbeck didn't believe in ghosts. And yet, there is also that long-told peninsula story about him having an exorcism performed at his Monterey home, the Lara Soto Adobe, before he would move in. A baby is said to have been buried near the large cyprus tree in front of the Lara Soto Adobe. This might explain the muffled cries that are sometimes heard in the building. We can only wonder what Steinbeck may have sensed regarding the adobe. He only lived there for a year, while working on *The Pearl*.

In her book *My Life with John Steinbeck*, Gwyn Conger Steinbeck claims that John was a mystic who did not believe in reincarnation, but did indeed believe in ghosts.

A few guild members have admitted to having seen the ghostly Steinbeck, or having felt him brush past them as if he were in some kind of hurry. None have been frightened by the apparition. Patrons that have seen him say he is not ominous and merely watches from afar; certainly nothing to ruin a superb meal over. Another ghostly resident in the house may be that of Steinbeck's mother, who is most often spotted at the top of the stairs.

Hotel San Carlos

While many of Monterey's historic buildings are still standing, progress sealed the fate of others. Among those that were razed was the elegant old Hotel San Carlos that stood on the corner of Franklin and Calle Principal. Once of the peninsula's premier addresses, the San Carlos counted Billie Holiday, Marilyn Monroe, and John Steinbeck among its famous guests. It's prime real estate; when the bulldozers were finished with the San Carlos, the Monterey Sheridan (the Marriot now) was built.

Perhaps this marked the end of the ghostly little girl that was so often seen at the goldfish pond in front of the Hotel San Carlos. Then again, it's possible that she may still be there, a little specter out of time, taking delight in the sparkling goldfish that swim the length of a long-ago pond. Who can say?

Bodie, a Real Ghost Town

*B*odie is a ghost town and also happens to be a California Historic State Park. Located near Bridgeport, Bodie is usually California's coldest spot during the winter. That's perfect for a ghost, not so much for the living. In 1861 thousands of men and women began coming to Bodie in the hopes of striking it rich. Some of them had first come to California during the 1848–1855 gold rush.

Those who hadn't found gold packed up their families and headed for the eastern slope of the Sierra, and another chance. But Bodie was not a family town. From the beginning, it was known as a wild town; not a safe place to live. And yet, blinded by gold, they came.

According to an often-told legend, a young girl, when told her family was moving to Bodie, wrote in a letter, "Goodbye God, we're going to Bodie."

Newspapers across the country found humor, if not wisdom, in the words and reprinted them for their readers' enjoyment. Only Bodie newspapers balked. It was all in the punctuation. According to the Bodie newspapers, what the child had actually written was, "Good. By God we're going to Bodie."

Good for a laugh, but life was especially hard on the children of Bodie. They were subjected to the same harsh winters and the violence that the adults were. Then, too, there was rampaging disease and accidents doomed many of the town's youngsters to early graves.

As a town, Bodie was a flash in the pan. By the early twentieth century, many families had picked up and moved away. But it would take a little boy playing with matches to send the town into a decline from which it would never recover. On a summer morning in June 1932 a two-and-a-half-year-old boy known as Bodie Bill was playing with matches out back of a Main Street saloon. The devastation was swift. Within minutes dozens of buildings lay in ashes. Little Bill was unscathed, but his handiwork created the most disastrous fire in Bodie's history. There would be no rebuilding. The boom was finally over. The mines had closed and businesses had relocated elsewhere. Most of Bodie's citizens followed suit. By the early 1950s the last of Bodie's residents had packed up and moved on.

That's when the vandals and scavengers came, hauling away anything they considered valuable. This is when the State of California stepped in to take Bodie under its protective wing. The old ghost town is now a state historic park, putting an end to the vandalism that would have destroyed Bodie. Today photographers, history buffs, Wild West enthusiasts, and ghosthunters can still enjoy many of the old mining town's buildings and artifacts that are left in what the park terms "a state of arrested decay."

About an hour's drive from the east gate of Yosemite, Bodie is one of the West's best preserved ghost towns. It is visited by thousands of tourists each year, lured by stories of the wanton red-light district, cold-blooded gunslingers, and the ghosts who wander the old windblown cemetery. The last person buried in the Bodie Cemetery was Robert "Bobby" Bell, who was laid to rest on June 18, 2003. His epitaph reads, *Hello God; I've just arrived from Bodie. I am the last of the old time miners.*

Bodie is only open to tourists during daylight hours. Although the park is open during the winter months, tourists seldom visit then. This is still a hostile land. Temperatures sometimes drop to twenty or more below zero. Winter snowstorms have been known to dump fifteen feet of snow in the area making it impossible for all but snowmobiles to get in and out of Bodie. And this is when Bodie becomes inhabitable only to its ghosts.

Bodie's Namesake

*M*iners were superstitious. One superstition had it that anyone who discovered a rich producing ore vein was destined to meet a tragic death. In the case of Bill Bodey it was true. Bodey was one of four prospectors who crossed the Sonora Pass in the summer of 1859 in search of gold. Bodey had come to California during the gold rush, leaving behind a wife and family in faraway Poughkeepsie, New York. Perhaps he hoped to return to them one day, perhaps not. Either way, he struck pay dirt with the discovery of gold on the eastern slope of the Sierra Nevada Mountains.

Bodey and his partners were ecstatic. They named the site and set themselves up a campsite that included a small cabin. With fall closing in the four agreed it was best to return to Monoville and to keep their discovery secret until the spring. But Bodey didn't keep his word. In Monoville, he wasted little time in talking a man by the name of Black Taylor into returning to the cabin with him. When greed kicks in it's difficult to say no. And so Bodey and Taylor remained working in the area. As their food supply dwindled they decided to set out on foot for Monoville and fresh supplies. But they hadn't reckoned on an early winter storm.

Halfway back to the campsite the two men were overcome by a raging blizzard. As they fought to find their way to the cabin, Bodey fell to the ground exhausted.

"Come on, man. Get up! We're not that far away," Taylor coaxed.

Bodey pulled himself up and stumbled on a few more yards then fell helplessly in the snow. Taylor lifted him up and carried him on his shoulders. But he was as disoriented as Bodey. He had no idea where the cabin was or how far away they were from it. He stopped and placed Bodey in the snow. "It's just up there a bit. I'll come back for you in a bit." If Bodey heard him, he gave no sign. And Taylor trudged on. The luck that had deserted Bill Bodey was with him. Somehow he managed to find the cabin and light a fire. While he warmed himself, he thought of his friend out in the snowstorm somewhere. Was it the howling of the wind at the door, or the haunted cries of Bodey that kept him awake most of the night? He could never be quite sure.

The next morning Taylor trudged out into the snow and found the body of Bill Bodey. After burying his friend, he made his way back to the cabin and tried to live life as usual. But it wasn't to be. Night after night, the dead and buried Bodey cried out to him for help.

Bodey could not rest in peace. His remains were discovered by J. G. McClinton in 1871 and in 1879 McClinton and Joseph Wasson exhumed Bodey for reburial in the town cemetery. The November 3, 1879, issue of the *Bodie Chronicle* reported:

> On Sunday last Judge McClinton and Joe Wasson went to the grave of Williams S. Bodey and commenced exhuming the remains of the pioneer whose name is bestowed upon the town of Bodie. The remains having been discovered, operations were suspended until the following day, when, in the presence of several citizens they were removed and brought to town. The much mooted question as to the location of the grave has thus been settled. There was found the skull, a few bones, gun, necktie, bowie knife, shoe button, blanket and cloth. His remains will be reinterred tomorrow afternoon at 3 O'clock, under the auspices of the Pacific Coast Pioneers of Bodie. A general invitation is extended to citizens to attend.

Bill Bodey had not lived long enough to enjoy the honor of having a town named after him, or to correct the misspelling of his namesake town. He may have been happy to realize that thanks to his 1859 discovery, more prospectors would come into the region and Bodie's population would soar to nearly ten thousand citizens. But then again, considering that many of them were ruthless gunslingers and lawless hombres, he may not have been.

About that misspelling: One story has it that the town's fathers didn't want anyone to mispronounce the name of their town and call it Body. This was at a time when Victoria ruled Britain and her straitlaced mores ruled the rest of the world. So to guard against any such vulgar faux pas, they changed the spelling. It was all good. Still you've got to wonder what Queen Victoria might have said about Bodie's red-light district.

Some lay the misspelling on the paints and brushes of a local sign painter. He got the spelling wrong and the name stuck.

All Those Ghosts

*I*f you're counting different ghosts, then the Cain House on the corner of Green and Park Streets is one of the most active in Bodie. There's a ghostly old woman who rocks away eternity in the glass-enclosed front porch. Silently she rocks back and forth, to and fro, in the ancient rocking chair. Her housemates from the hereafter include the ghost of a beautiful Chinese woman and that of a middle-aged matron.

James Stuart (J. S.) Cain made his fortune in Bodie selling lumber that he barged across Mono Lake. Without any nearby timber sources, he had a booming market. The more the mines boomed, the more lumber was needed. He came to Bodie at age twenty-five and within a few years he was one of the town's movers and shakers, as in a wealthy mine owner and real estate owner. In the end, the Cain family owned Bodie, lock, stock, and yes, the cemetery too. In the late 1950s talks between the Cains and the State began in earnest. Eventually a deal was struck and the State of California became the rightful owner of the ghost town.

Rumor has it that the ghostly Chinese woman once worked as a housekeeper for Mr. and Mrs. Cain. It's a story as old as the Bodie Hills themselves. An attraction grew between Mr. Cain and the housekeeper. Soon a romantic fling was going on right there in the Cain home. But just as old as the Bodie Hills is a wife's sixth sense about such matters. Mrs. Cain was no fool. While J. S. was forgiven, the housekeeper was sent packing.

Shamed in the Chinese community, the young woman couldn't find work anywhere else. In desperation she took her own life. But as any ghost researcher will tell you, suicides can end up as ghosts who linger for a very long time. Apparently, she has. Her apparition has been seen at the Cain House almost since the first day she swallowed poison. And her ghost is still angry about the unfairness of it all. Understandably, she reportedly adores children, but has no use for grown-ups. Adults who have slept in the Cain House say they've seen her. One person woke with the feeling of someone sitting on her and trying to crush her. She wrestled with the ghost and ended up on the floor. Other strange goings on at the Cain House are doors that open and close of their own volition. No, it's not the wind.

The matron is believed to be the wife of Jesse McGrath, the original builder of the Cain House. Several people have seen her standing in the upstairs bedroom where she died. No one is afraid of her. Obviously, she means no harm. Still, it can be a bit disconcerting to wake and see some frump in a long-ago frock staring down at you. As to the elderly rocking chair rider, it's anybody's guess who she was and why she has chosen to stay on here at the Cain House.

When the sun goes down, the shimmering apparition of a child appears in the old Bodie Cemetery. The ghostly child playing among the old marble headstones is Evelyn Myers, known as the Angel of Bodie; she is Bodie's most famous ghost, and while she has also been seen in town, she prefers the cemetery where countless other of Bodie's residents now rest.

Over years of retellings, some of Evelyn's story has been altered or lost. The miner, who plays a key role in her death, may have been a friend of the family who gave her the attention her parents didn't. Every morning Evelyn waited outside her small house until she heard the miner's cheerful whistle. Then off she went, tagging along behind him. Once he got to his job site, she would crouch nearby and watch him go about his chores, before heading back home.

On the morning of her death, winds began whipping down the Sierra. Overhead the sky was thick with clouds and the threat of a snowstorm. Evelyn wasn't aware of the impending storm as she followed closely on the miner's heels. But he had lived on the eastern slope of the Sierra long enough to know the signs. It was early spring; still this was not a day for a child to be playing outdoors. He stopped and told Evelyn to go back home. She frowned and turned back toward town. Smiling to himself, he watched her go.

But Evelyn fooled him. She sneaked back, hid in the brush, and waited. When he was occupied with his task, she crept closer. She was within inches of him, and still he was unaware of her. Suddenly he swung his heavy pickaxe backward, smashing it into Evelyn's head and killing her instantly.

Her parents were devastated. The miner and the townspeople were so heartbroken at the unfortunate death that they erected a guardian angel tombstone for Evelyn. People from all over the world come to Bodie to photograph Evelyn's angel and to lay flowers at her gravesite. Countless people have encountered the ghostly Evelyn herself, flitting among the sagebrush and the headstones.

While these experiences usually occur after dark, I will tell you about a recent ghostly experience I had during daylight hours. It was an unusually hot summer day in Bodie. After walking through town, Bill and I set out to visit the cemetery and to photograph little Evelyn's headstone. While I wandered alone through one section of the cemetery in search of the headstone, Bill walked another, several yards distant.

I spoke softly to the little girl, wishing her happiness on the other side. I told her that although I'd visited her grave before, I couldn't remember exactly where it was and hoped that she would guide me there.

Suddenly I heard a group of women approaching me. As they laughed and talked, I stopped speaking, hoping they hadn't heard me out here talking to a ghost. I stopped and waited for them to walk past me, ready with a cheery "Good morning."

I waited . . . and waited. No one approached. I looked around; there was no one here in this section with me, except Bill.

"What happened to those women I heard?"

"What women?" he asked.

"It sounded like there were three or four of them," I explained.

"I didn't see anyone but you here," he said.

"Did you hear them?"

"I didn't hear anything," he answered.

Had the sounds of people walking in the town area been carried by the wind . . . or had I heard a group of ghosts happily making their way back to their final resting places? A skeptic will say it was the wind. And it may well have been—but I doubt it.

Ghost researchers maintain that a sudden, unexpected death is one reason for ghostly activity—that and tragedy. And if anyone's life was tragic it was that of the unfortunate Lottie Johl.

The Johl House is still there on Main Street. Thousands of photographs have been taken of the house and its once elegant parlor with its sewing machine, piano, and ornate stove. Look closely. Occasionally the ghostly Lottie Johl makes an appearance in the dust-covered rooms. She's also said to wander the streets of Bodie in a glowing white gown. Certainly she's not a happy ghost, but why should she be? If anyone was born to endless night it was Lottie.

Once she moved into Bodie's red-light district, known as Virgin Alley, Lottie faced the community's cruelty and scorn. She had come here fleeing a bad marriage and worse, divorce; she had no illusions. Lottie had convinced herself that love was only a word bandied about when the mood struck. She was young. But not so young that she was looking for love. Because she had youth and beauty on her side, she went to work in the High Grade, one of Bodie's top brothels. Like the bartenders, the miners, the school teacher, and the newspaper reporters, she was here to earn a living.

It wasn't long before she caught the eye of Eli Johl, the town's butcher, there in the High Grade's parlor. He was smitten. She was interested. He showered her with kindness and expensive gifts and she found herself falling in love with him. As they got to know each other better, Eli decided that yes, she would make a wonderful wife. And so he proposed. He had the money to back up his promises to her. The shop he and Charles Donnelly owned was one of the most successful in town. She had never been happier. At last she was to have a normal life.

They married and settled into a lavishly furnished five-room home on Main Street. In another time or place Lottie may have ended up being a great patron of the arts or celebrated hostess, but this was nineteenth-century Bodie and the town was outraged, particularly its female citizens. There were no second chances for women like Lottie. Men could kill each other over the slightest provocation in one of the saloons, but how dare Eli Johl marry such a tarnished woman and set her up to live among the town's *decent* people? Leading the charge against Lottie was none other than Annie Donnelly, the wife of Eli's business partner.

Even when Eli and Lottie planned a wonderful party in celebration of their marriage, Annie Donnelly managed to convince everyone to stay away. So there the heartbroken Johls sat, amidst all the delicacies Lottie had prepared, at a party without guests. And the treatment would continue. Day in, day out, no one came calling at the Johl home. It's anybody's guess here in the twenty-first century why the Johls didn't just pack up and relocate elsewhere where Lottie's past would not torment her. But they didn't. And Lottie suffered an unimaginable loneliness in her fine home while Eli was working at his butcher shop.

Worried about her, Eli bought her some paints, brushes, and canvases. She would be an artist, he reasoned. Today one of her paintings hangs in the museum at Bodie, a lonely mountain landscape with a lake and tall pines. What thoughts ran through her mind as she wielded the brush on that long-ago day? Was this a scene painted from memory, or did it spring from her imagination?

Eli was determined that Bodie would see the goodness in Lottie. While he worked at the butcher shop, Eli tried to find ways for that to happen. If only they knew her gentleness, her kindness. Then as if in answer to his prayers, there was an article in the paper. The town was a buzz with plans for a masquerade ball. Everyone would be there. And there would be a prize for the best costume. *Aha*, thought Eli. *This will be Lottie's chance to shine.*

Lottie was more skeptical. She had seen the cruelty shining in the eyes of the other women, but she was willing to try, if only to please Eli. After talking it over for days, they agreed on an exquisite costume, a beautiful white satin dress that shimmered with rhinestones and seed pearls. They laughed like children as they spent their evenings making plans for the big event. How could society deny Lottie when they saw what a wonderful dancer she was? Who could fail to notice how gracefully she moved and how lovely she was in her costume? As Eli assured her that this was the moment they had hoped for, she silently wished him to be right.

And so, the evening arrived. Lottie dressed so carefully and checked her reflection in the mirror again and again. Eli hovered. "Schön!" he exclaimed.

"Oh yes Eli, it is a beautiful dress."

"No, it is you who are beautiful," he corrected her with a smile.

So that no one would know her identity until the midnight unmasking, Lottie went alone to the Miners Union Hall. And just as she and Eli had envisioned, she was the belle of the ball. Everyone wanted to dance with the lady in the shimmering white gown. *At last,* Lottie told herself. The past was behind her. She could take her place in polite society. Mrs. Lottie Johl, wife of the town butcher. Her imagination drifted from one idea to the next. She and Eli would throw extravagant parties. Then she would show these people all the paintings she had created. They would gasp when they saw that her paintings were just as good, if not better than those of Annie Donnelly. And they would be her friends. She smiled. With friends she might not be painting as much.

A sip of champagne, another compliment on her costume, and another dance; the hours whirled away. It was midnight and time for the best costume to be announced. She had won! Eli would be thrilled. Now for the unmasking; she pulled her mask off with a smile. "See me? I'm not what you thought!"

The room was silent. "You've got your nerve," someone whispered in her ear. "Do us all a favor and leave at once."

As she ran sobbing along the dusty street, the hem of her gown dragged in the dirt, her hairpins fell out one by one, and myriad stars blazed overhead. All their plans had been for naught. These people would never accept her.

She was a disheveled, wild woman by the time she walked through the door. Eli was furious as she sobbed out her horror and humiliation. But he was powerless against the narrow-minded nineteenth-century caste that controlled Bodie's social structure. And he knew it. Never again would Lottie allow herself to hope for a normal life. Never again would she try to gain their acceptance. There would be no social calls, parties, or friendships. It was just the two of them.

The years passed. The butcher shop prospered, Lottie continued painting, and life fell into a comfortable routine. Then came the day Lottie just didn't feel herself. She went to bed earlier than usual, but was still exhausted the next morning. Eli brought the doctor to examine her. "It is nothing serious," he assured the anxious husband. "Some rest and—" he scribbled out a prescription. "This ought to help."

Ever mindful of his wife's comfort, Eli dashed to the pharmacy and back. He had Lottie's medicine. And soon she would be her old self. But there is something about being born to endless night . . . the bad luck never stops. Lottie rose up on one elbow and sipped from the glass Eli held. Then she swallowed the pills. Hours later she was writhing in pain . . . and then she was gone.

The talk was swift—and cruel: Lottie Johl committed suicide. Her past had finally caught up with her. Eli ordered an autopsy to quell the rumors. Lottie had been poisoned—a horrible mistake. The pharmacist had gotten medicine and poison mixed up. In today's world the pharmacist would pay dearly, to the tune of millions, for such a dreadful mistake. But this was the nineteenth century. There would be no lawsuit. Besides, Eli had other things on his mind, like where Lottie was to be buried.

Even in death, they held her past against her. Lottie, they said, should not rest within the gates with them, but outside with the other immoral red-light women. Some took sides with Eli. Lottie was his wife. She had proven herself a true and loyal woman, after all. Finally it was decided that Lottie could be buried in the cemetery, but at a distance away.

It is this strong sense of injustice that has kept the specter of Lottie Johl wandering the abandoned streets of Bodie in her glowing white gown, something she was never permitted to do in life. When she tires of this the ghostly Lottie returns to her once beautiful home on Main Street.

We saw her in there, bent over the sewing machine. It was broad daylight and she turned and nodded. We assumed she was a docent. We later found out she wasn't.

Ghosts don't always show themselves. Aside from speaking out with disembodied voices, they've been known to announce their presence with a distinctive aroma. Some examples are a long-dead lady's perfume, the fragrance of a favorite flower, and the aroma of cooking. The smell of freshly grated garlic and Italian food are said to emanate from The Mendocini House. Mangia! Mangia! Apparently, a ghostly mom and her brood haunt the place.

Before you tuck in, you should know that they've all been known to tag along behind those they've taken a liking to. But once the visit is over and the visitor is settled safely in his or her car, it's arrivederci from mama and the kids. The ghostly gourmands are back to their own haunted abode and more good eats.

Put food out of your mind and think of this. There's a house over on Fuller Street where the body of a young woman was disemboweled, diced, and dissected, all in the name of science. By the flickering light of candles and kerosene, the doctor went about his gruesome work. Ugh! The unmistakable smell of embalming fluid, 1880s-style formaldehyde, and that's enough to curb any appetite. And that brings us to the unfortunate Mary Turner.

Dr. Blackwood and the
Corpse of Mary Turner

*T*he Old West had its share of haunted mine-shaft stories. So many miners perished while working deep within them that there were bound to be a few ghosts lurking about. One ghost, who may be residing deep within the old Champion Mine at Bodie, California, didn't die there. In fact she didn't descend its depths until long after she was dead.

On December 8, 1881, the wind that had come howling down off the Sierra was silent now. All across Bodie snow lay in knee-deep drifts. Filled with timber, the old woodstove kept the room warmed comfortably. As she lay dying, nineteen-year-old Mary Turner barely noticed. In those last moments of life neither she nor her husband could have imagined what horrors awaited. She gazed lovingly at him, and took her last breath. They took Mary's body to the undertakers, where she would be prepared for her trip to the cemetery. After the briefest of ceremonies, she was consigned to the nearly frozen earth.

A week later the night watchman at the Champion Mine saw two men toss a large box down into the Ajax shaft. Always on the lookout for a story, a newspaper reporter who heard about the incident agreed to accompany the watchman down into the shaft. Together they would retrieve whatever it was that was thrown down there.

What they discovered there in the depths was horrific. Female body parts. . . first a hand and then a thigh, a torso, and a head; what sort of monster was responsible, they wondered.

Mr. Turner hadn't a clue. But the description fit that of his recently departed Mary. When the recovered remains were put on display at Brown's Undertaking Room, he joined those who were taking ghoulish delight in the spectacle. It could be Mary. But there was really only one way to tell. And sure enough, when he and friends dug up her coffin, Mary wasn't resting in peace within its confines. Who was responsible? Fingers started pointing.

First at this one, then at that; finally a man claimed he had gotten the dead woman's body for Dr. Blackwood. There in the privacy of a secret location on Fuller Street, Dr. Blackwood lowered the shades, lit the kerosene lamps, and used the body of Mary for his personal study of cadavers. How else could one learn?

The February 27, 1882, edition of the *Reno Evening Gazette* carried a story titled "Horrible Story." The following is excerpted from that story:

> The Coroner's Jury, after long and tedious examination of obstinate and unwilling witnesses, traced the remains found to Dr. Blackwood, who either dug them up himself or hired the disagreeable word done. He rented a vacant house on Fuller Street for the purpose (it is believed) and dissected the body of the late Mrs. Turner. The skull found its way to Dr. Jones' office, and a competent lady witness testified that she recognized the same as the skull of Mrs. Turner by the teeth, which were remarkably even and handsome. One witness testified that he frequently accompanied Dr. Blackwood to the dissecting room, and saw him use a knife on the remains, cutting away flesh and performing other work in that direction. The man who so testified was one of the unwilling witnesses, but the circumstances were such that he was forced to disgorge a portion of his knowledge regarding the affair. Dr. Blackwood testified that he knew nothing about the remains, and then jumped the town and has not yet been overtaken.

The evidence was stacked against him, but the good doctor denied it all. Mary, or what remained of her, was gathered up and reburied in the Bodie Cemetery. Dr. Blackwood left town never to be seen again in Bodie. And Mary Turner? She walks a lonely path through Bodie on those long winter nights when the snow is piled deep.

The Wandering Madame Moustache Ghost

*I*n her youth Eleanor Dumont was a beautiful prostitute who plied her trade all over the West. As she aged, Dumont found she could make more money in a high-stakes card game than in a brothel. So she traveled across the West gambling, and generally winning it all. Somewhere along the way she became known as Madame Moustache. Some said it was because of the dark hairs that sprouted above her lip. Others insisted it was because she intensely disliked men with moustaches. Either way the sobriquet stuck.

Madame Moustache was a formidable player. Only those who didn't mind losing dared to sit in on the same game. But luck can turn in an instant. And Dumont's did. She arrived in Bodie in 1878. Backed by a borrowed stake, she anted up in a poker game at the Grand Central Saloon. The cards were dealt. Dumont's was a bad hand. No amount of whiskey could warm the cold streak she was riding.

She left the saloon in debt and out of hope. Suicide seemed her only answer. And so she walked along the road toward Bridgeport until she was about two miles outside of Bodie. It was the end of the road for her. She stopped and took a gulp of poison. Eleanor Dumont aka Madame Moustache died where she fell. The newspaper reported her death:

The Bodie Morning News September 9, 1879

A Suicide—Yesterday morning a sheep-herder, while in pursuit of his avocation, discovered the dead body of a woman lying about one hundred yards from the Bridgeport road, a mile from town. Her head rested on a stone, and the appearance of the body indicated that death was the result of natural causes. Ex-officio

Coroner Justice Peterson was at once notified, and he dispatched a wagon in charge of H.Ward [of the Pioneer Furniture Store] to that place, who brought the body to the undertaking rooms. Deceased was named Eleanore Dumont, and was recognized as the woman who had been engaged in dealing a twenty-one game in the Magnolia saloon. Her death evidently occurred from an overdose of morphine, an empty bottle having the peculiar smell of that drug, being found beside the body. . . . The history connected with the unfortunate suicide is but a repetition of that of many others who have followed the life of a female gambler, with the exception perhaps that the subject of this item bore a character for virtue possessed by few in her line. To the goodhearted women of the town must we accord praise for their accustomed kindness in doing all in their power to prepare the unfortunate woman's body for burial.

They buried her in the outcast section of the Bodie Cemetery, and forgot about her. Her beleaguered ghost is reportedly encountered at dusk, walking the same road she died on. Death has revitalized her. Those who've seen her claim that Eleanor Dumont is an attractive young woman, without a hint of the hirsuteness she was noted for in life.

La Llorona

The legend of La Llorona (the Weeping Woman) is known throughout California and the Southwest. In the first printed mention of La Llorona, Mexican writer Manuel Carpio wrote a poem about her in the late 1800s. Carpio made no mention of her having killed her children, but that she was cruelly murdered by her faithless husband. There are as many versions of La Llorona as there are beads on the mantilla she is said to wear.

Believed to be the apparition of a once beautiful woman who murdered her children so that she could run away with her lover, seeing La Llorona is never a good omen. Some say to see her is to die. And given the chance, she will steal children and take them away so that they are never seen again. In one favorite version of the La Llorona tale, her lover gave her an ultimatum: me or your kids. Sadly, she chose him.

In order to free herself of her responsibility, she dragged her small children to the river and drowned them in the rushing waters. But her happiness was short lived. Her lover's attention soon turned toward another woman, and he abandoned La Llorona. This is when she realized what she'd done. And she went mad with the knowledge that she'd murdered her children for a man who cared for no one but himself.

Dressed in her one good lace dress she drank poison as a way of atoning for her terrible sin. She died an agonizing death. But there would be no resting in peace for her. Shortly after her burial in a pauper's grave, people began to see La Llorona, dressed in her tattered lace dress and mantilla, walking forlornly along the banks of the river bank and wailing loudly.

Yet another version of the legend has La Llorona and her children murdered by her husband so that he can be free to wed another.

She walks along the water's edge hoping to exact revenge for the long-ago murder.

No one wants to hear her wailing; no one wants to come face to face with La Llorona. And no one dares speak her name aloud. To do so, it is whispered, invites evil into one's life. She is described by some as a haggard, witch-like woman with burning coals as eyes. Others say she is as beautiful in death as she was in life. Either way, it is never a good idea to stand between La Llorona and the water.

Mission San Carlos Borromeo de Carmelo

Still, by peasants at Carmelo,
Tales are told and songs are sung,
Of Junipero, the Padre,
In the sweet Castilian tongue,
Telling how each year he rises
From his grave the Mass to say.
In the midnight, mid the ruins,
On the eve of San Carlo's day . . .

—Richard Edward White
from the 1890 poem "Midnight Mass"

In 1769 Father Junipero Serra and Don Gaspar de Portola were sent by Spain on a threefold mission: to enforce Spain's claim on Alta California (present-day California), to build missions and presidios (fortified military settlements), and to instruct the indigenous people in Christianity and Spanish culture.

On June 3, 1770, Father Junipero Serra and Gaspar de Portola founded the city of Monterey and the Carmel Mission, the second mission to be built in California. This building known as the San Carlos Chapel and the Royal Presidio Chapel still stands today. And yes, there is a ghost story here. There is the candle that seems to float on its own volition inside the chapel when no one is about. The brightly lit candle is said to be held by the unseen hands of a long-ago priest who appears only briefly as he makes his way toward the rectory. Then there is the pealing of bells that emanate from the old chapel and are occasionally heard in the wee hours of the morning.

But Father Junipero Serra (who was granted sainthood in 2015) was not satisfied with the location. Although the mission was within a mile of Monterey Bay, in the safety of the presidio and the capital city, he realized that the Native Americans he wished to convert were living nearby in a better location for farming and fishing and a fresh water source.

In August 1771, the Carmel Mission was moved to present-day Carmel. Father Junipero Serra would be in charge of the mission from 1770 until his death in 1784. The beloved saint is buried in the sanctuary at the mission. Among those who are buried outside in the mission's courtyard cemetery is Old Gabriel, whose headstone claims that he was 151 years old when he died in 1890. Old Gabriel could well be the ghostly stooped old man who reportedly roams the courtyard during the summer months.

Father Junipero Serra's canonization in 2015 did not come without some controversy. While Serra is the patron saint of California, there are those who strongly disagree with his sainthood because of the harsh treatment Native Americans were subjected to under his rule.

In Richard Edward White's poem, Father Junipero Serra returns to the mission on San Carlos Day (November 4), but others say he actually returns to the mission on Christmas Eve. Others insist he never leaves. Visitors have told of seeing a ghostly gray-clad man in several locations throughout the mission. This, they say, is Saint Junipero Serra keeping watch over his beloved Mission San Carlos Borromeo de Carmelo.

The Ghost of Arana Gulch

*A*rana Gulch is a designated greenbelt on Santa Cruz's east side; many endangered species thrive here. One might not expect to find a ghost, but on nights when the fog sweeps in off the bay, the ghost of Arana Gulch floats across the tall eucalyptus trees. Wearing a long black coat and wide brimmed black hat, the ghost is that of Andrew Jackson "Jack" Sloan who was murdered here on a long-ago Saturday night in 1865. The death was unexpected. And although fate eventually caught up with them, the killers were never brought to justice. Those are two very good reasons for a haunting to occur.

On February 11, 1865, a full moon hung gloriously in the night sky. Jack Sloan and his brother-in-law John Towne finished their dinner at a Santa Cruz café and were on their way to their farm at Rodeo Gulch. The two men chatted amicably as they rode along Old Soquel Road not knowing that one of them was headed toward his doom.

Under the bridge at Arana Gulch, Joe Rodriguez and Pedro and Faustino Lorenzana were lying in wait for John Arana, who they'd fought with at a recent dance. When they realized Arana had seen them and made an escape, they angrily made a pact to kill the next man who crossed the bridge.

The men were Jack Sloan and John Towne. Joe Rodriguez grabbed the bridle of Sloan's horse as they started across the bridge. "Where are you two men headed?" Rodriguez demanded.

"Not your business," Sloan replied.

This was not the reply Rodriguez was expecting. He angrily seethed as Sloan and Towne urged their horses to full speed. When they were a safe distance away, the two men stopped. "I'm going back to give those men a good piece of my mind," Jack said.

"There are three of them. Let's just go on," Towne said.

But Jack Sloan wasn't listening. He raced his horse back to the men.

"Who are you three, hombres?" he demanded, as he came upon them once again.

"Not your business," Rodriguez smirked.

This infuriated Sloan, who began hitting the men with a rope. Rodriguez lunged for Sloan, pulling him off his horse. Sloan struck Rodriguez in the face. Rodriguez angrily pulled his pistol and shot Sloan twice in the stomach.

Arriving at the scene, Towne tried desperately to help Sloan. Rodriguez and the Lorenzanas jumped on their horses and made their escape. Towne summoned help. But it was too late for Andrew Jackson Sloan. He died there in Arana Gulch for no good reason, angry and alone.

Thirty years later on June 25, 1895, the *Santa Cruz Daily Sentinel* carried an article titled "Saw an Apparition." It told of a woman and her daughter who were driving their buggy home through Arana Gulch one evening. As they approached the spot where Jack Sloan was murdered, the tall thin specter of a man in a long black coat and a wide brimmed hat, crossed in front of them. They were so frightened of the ghost that they raced the buggy into Santa Cruz to share their story.

Thereafter the ghost of Jack Sloan began making regular visits to Arana Gulch. And he may well do so to this day.

Lone Pine's Rescue Man on Whitney Portal Road

If you've ever watched a Western or a sci-fi movie, chances are a portion of it was filmed in the Alabama Hills near Lone Pine, a favorite location of filmmakers since the early 1920s. The ruggedly picturesque Alabama Hills is a range of rock formations and hills in the Owens Valley near the eastern slope of the Sierra Nevada.

Whitney Portal Road, which runs through the Alabama Hills, was featured in the 1941 film *High Sierra* and the 1954 Lucille Ball–Desi Arnaz comedy *The Long, Long Trailer*.

The road will take you halfway up Mount Whitney, the tallest mountain in the contiguous United States at 14,405 feet above sea level. It is here on Whitney Portal Road that the legend of Lone Pine's Rescue Man begins.

Several years after the California Gold Rush, gold was discovered in the Alabama Hills area sometime around 1860. It was nothing on the scale of James Marshall's discovery at Sutter's Mill, but it was enough to keep people prospecting the area in earnest for many years afterward. On a fall morning in 1940 a local prospector known as Indian Jim went out into the hills in search of gold. Ignoring the signs of an impending storm, he was caught in a sudden blizzard and lost his way. He perished there in subzero temperatures.

Two years later George, a friend of Jim's, was prospecting in the hills when Jim appeared before him. "George!" the ghostly Jim said.

Shocked at seeing his dead friend suddenly standing before him, George asked, "What do you want, Jim?"

"Go!" Jim demanded, pointing toward town. "Go now!"

George obeyed, practically running back to Lone Pine. It was a sound decision. A horrific blizzard descended on the area just as George walked through his front door. If not for Jim, he would have perished out in the Alabama Hills.

While some people are fearful of ghosts, there is something about Jim that people trust. Over the years he has become known as Rescue Man for the lives he's saved.

Headless in the Hereafter

*T*here's just something about a headless ghost. From the headless horseman of George Washington Irving's *Legend of Sleepy Hollow*, to the headless specter of Henry VIII's ill-fated second wife, Anne Boleyn, a ghost without his or her head demands immediate action. Run! What could be more frightening than going into the hereafter minus one's head?

In the Central Coast region of the Golden State three headless specters have been roaming the countryside for over a hundred years. The bandit Joaquin Murrieta is our first headless ghost. Murrieta and his wife came from Mexico seeking riches in the California gold rush. There was a lot of hatred for Mexicans in the California gold camps. One night a group of drunks broke into the Murrieta cabin, shot Murrieta, then raped and killed his wife. When he recovered, Joaquin Murrieta was never the same. Full of resentment toward the Americans, he turned to crime. Soon he fell in with a band of murdering thieves that were terrorizing all of central California.

But he hadn't counted on how far the California government would go to bring him to justice. In 1853 the California Rangers, California's statewide law enforcement agency, was created to rid the new state of ruthless bandits they called the Five Joaquins. In addition to Murrieta, the Five Joaquins included Joaquin Valenzuela, Joaquin Ocomorenia, Joaquin Carillo, and Joaquin Botellier. The Rangers believed Murrieta and these men were responsible for at least twenty murders and countless robberies in California's rich gold country.

After four of the men were hanged or captured, Joaquin Murrieta continued his banditry. Harry Love was appointed captain of the California Rangers and charged with hiring twenty men to help in stopping Murrieta. It took the Rangers two months, and then on

July 25, 1853, they caught up with Murrieta and his men. First to fall was Three Fingers Jack. And as one after another of his gang members fell dead in the ensuing gun battle, Murrieta mounted his horse and attempted to escape. Ranger Billy Henderson gave chase, yanking Murrieta off his horse. Murrieta pulled his pistol and fired. Henderson's aim was better. And Joaquin Murrieta lay dead in the dry grass. This wasn't good enough for Captain Love. He wanted proof.

In order to prove that the Rangers had accomplished their mission, he ordered the hand of Three Fingers Jack cut off and Murrieta decapitated. After which, the head was placed in a jar of bourbon. The head would be displayed in various bars and inns throughout central California until it ended up at a San Francisco museum. And there it would remain until the disastrous 1906 earthquake. Where is Joaquin Murrieta's head today? No one seems to know.

And this has caused a great deal of consternation to the ghost of Joaquin Murrieta, who has accosted many people asking, *"¿Dónde está mi cabeza?"* (Where is my head?)

One of the first people the headless Murrieta is said to have haunted was Billy Henderson. And, according to Major Horace Bell in his 1930 posthumously published book *On the Old West Coast*, the ghostly Joaquin Murrieta hounded Henderson for the rest of his life, always demanding his head. It is interesting to note that in 1927 Bell made the bold statement,

"In any country . . . except the United States, the operations of Joaquín Murrieta would be dignified by the title of revolution, and the leader with that of rebel chief."

And indeed, Joaquin Murrieta was considered a folk hero to his fellow Mexicans new to California who suffered cruelty and violence at the hands of some of the Americans.

And so his ghost wanders in the night asking, *"¿Dónde está mi cabeza?"*

Cruelty and violence are what a young Native American woman suffered at the hands of her husband when he caught her in the arms of another man. According to legend, her husband murdered the man and decapitated her, burying her body and her head in separate graves. She is the headless horsewoman who rides a large white stallion through the Jolon, Fort Hunter Ligget, and the Mission San Antonio de Padua areas. She comes in search of her head.

Many people have witnessed this apparition of the headless horsewoman who only rides on the darkest of nights, when nothing but a sliver of moon hangs in the sky. Some have even given chase. But her stallion is too fast.

And yet, there is another headless woman in the region. According to some, her name was Alice and she and her husband and baby were traveling to their homestead when they arrived at the Nacimiento River. Despite warnings that the water was too swift and deep, they urged their team of horses into the raging water. Their wagon was overturned; Alice was caught in the reins and decapitated, and her baby drowned. Like the headless horsewoman, Alice only appears on moonless nights, seeking her head and her baby.

Southern California

Ghosts of the Leonis Adobe

*M*iguel Leonis and his wife, Espiritu, are the ghosts most associated with the adobe that is one of the oldest former private residences in the state of California. Built in 1844, the Leonis Adobe is also known as one of the most haunted places in Calabasas.

The ghostly Miguel Leonis is most often seen at the front door of the adobe. His heavy-booted footsteps are sometimes heard in the adobe as well. The ghost of Espiritu has been seen standing near a dresser. At other times she makes her presence known by unexplained odors and noises like slamming doors and knocking on walls. She is believed to be the ethereal figure that stands at the top of the stairs and calls, "Chichita, Chichita."

Chichita was the nickname she called her granddaughter Maria Orsua.

An astute businessman, Miguel Leonis owned the adobe for over fifteen years, and during that time he increased his wealth so that he and Espiritu deserved a finer home. Toward that end, he renovated and enlarged the adobe. Leonis was killed in 1889 near Cahuenga Pass when his wagon overturned, fatally injuring him.

Espiritu had learned how to legally protect herself. She went to court to keep her rights to the adobe, and continued living in it until her death in 1909.

The Leonis Adobe was placed on the National Register of Historic Places in 1875.

The Millennium Biltmore
and the Black Dahlia

*T*he Los Angeles Biltmore opened on October 1, 1923, six years before the 1929 stock market crash that would throw the nation into the Great Depression. More than three thousand people attended the grand opening party. At that time the Biltmore was the largest hotel in the US west of Chicago. Italian artist Giovanni Battista Smeraldi, who worked at the White House and the Vatican, was commissioned to paint the hotel's main galleria and crystal ballroom ceilings. Smeraldi would spend seven months painting his murals on the frescoed ceilings. The Biltmore's walls were marble and Venetian crystal chandeliers provided light. No expense had been spared. Everyone had money in their pocket, especially Hollywood's glamourous set.

The Biltmore was also the site of the 1935 Academy Awards, where Clark Gable and Claudette Colbert walked off with best actor and actress awards for their roles in *It Happened One Night*. The awards ceremony would be held at the Biltmore four more times until 1942. It would be enough to firmly establish the hotel as a preferred place for stars to congregate. The luxurious hotel was a favorite of celebrities, gangsters, and politicians alike. During their 1964 tour of the US the Beatles stayed in the presidential suite. Four years earlier the Democratic convention elected John F. Kennedy as its nominee at the Biltmore.

Several movies have filmed scenes at the hotel since it opened. The first was Cecil B. DeMille's 1924 *Triumph*. Others include *Chinatown, Beverly Hills Cop, Ghostbusters,* and the 1937 version of *A Star is Born*. But what would a hotel be without a ghost?

The Millennium Biltmore, as it's now called, has its share. The ghostly nurse is said to haunt the hotel's second floor. A startled guest woke one night to see a glowing woman at the foot of her bed.

Dressed in a nurse's uniform of the 1940s, complete with cap, the ghostly woman shook the foot of the bed as if trying to rouse someone, then turned and walked through the wall. The apparition has been seen numerous times walking the hallways of the second floor.

Some say the ghost of a little girl haunts the ninth-floor hallways. Others say she is not a child at all, but a ghostly young woman who giddily walks the hallways of the ninth floor, seemingly unaware that she is not of this world. Those who've encountered her say she seems to have imbibed too much bubbly. Perhaps she attended the party that goes on and on in the first-floor ballroom. Listen! You can hear the sounds of laughter and of tinkling glasses and of music from another era—this, even when the ballroom is empty.

But it is the unsolved murder of Elizabeth (Betty) Short that brought the hotel a lasting ghost story. Betty Short, aka the Black Dahlia, is the hotel's most famous ghost. She was young and beautiful. Those who knew her best said she was lazy and lacked direction, but she was trying to get her life on the right track. She never got the chance. Betty Short met the wrong person at the Biltmore Hotel in downtown Los Angeles on the night of January 9, 1947. Six days later her bisected body was discovered in a vacant lot of a Los Angeles neighborhood. All of a sudden she was famous—more famous than she ever could have imagined. But for all the wrong reasons. Newspaper reporters began calling her the Black Dahlia. Who did she meet? And why was she murdered?

And that leaves the Black Dahlia ghost who's been seen on the tenth floor by countless people. She never smiles or acknowledges anyone; she seems to be frightened and looking for someone. There is also the story of a man who rode the elevator with a beautiful dark-haired woman. Neither said a word to each other as the elevator made its way to the ground floor. She got off first and was gone before he realized which direction she went. It was only later when he saw a photo of her that he realized he'd shared the elevator with the Black Dahlia ghost.

Although countless people were questioned by detectives, the Black Dahlia's killer was never apprehended. With the passage of time, chances are good he never will be. This injustice alone is enough to cause a restless spirit to seek justice. And this may be what the beautiful ghost lady in black is trying to do at the Millennium Biltmore. Ponder that with a house-specialty Black Dahlia cocktail at the Millennium Biltmore's Gallery Bar.

Point Vicente Lighthouse

*W*hat a spectacular view the Point Vicente Lighthouse in Rancho Palos Verdes affords those who visit. This may seem like the perfect reason for a ghostly lighthouse keeper to linger. However, the ghost of the Point Vicente Lighthouse wasn't the former lighthouse keeper. She was said to be the ghost of a woman whose long-ago lover died in a shipwreck that happened here years before sailors petitioned to have a lighthouse, and long before that lighthouse was built in 1926.

She was here in search of her lost lover. Another story held that she was the wife of a lighthouse keeper who stumbled on the cliffs and fell to her death. Every night her apparition appeared in the tower room's opaque windows of the lighthouse. Dressed in a long white nightgown she danced round and round the room in a state of panic. She was called the Lady of the Light. And then in 1955 the windows were painted with a thicker paint—gone was their opacity. And that was the last anyone saw of the ghostly Lady of the Light in the tower room.

Her ghost, they say, still walks the nearby steep cliffs hoping to be reunited with her lover.

La Golondrina

*T*here is no place better than a haunted café. Actually, can you think of a better place for a ghost to hang out than in a restaurant that serves authentic and tasty Mexican dishes? I can't either. But the food is probably not the reason that the ghostly señora, known as La Consuela, haunts La Golondrina on Olvera Street in Los Angeles. Housed in the Pelanconi House, a firebrick building that was built by Italian vintner Guiseppi Covaccichi in 1857, it is the oldest such building in the city of Los Angles and a landmark.

The house was sold to Antonio Pelanconi in 1871 and the building is known as the Pelanconi House to this day. The historic three-story building has been the La Golondrina restaurant since 1930, the first Mexican restaurant in Los Angeles.

Apparently the ghostly La Consuela has decided to stay on indefinitely. She is usually seen in the stairwell, at an upstairs window, or on the balcony. Dressed in white, she is believed to be responsible for things that fly through the air, cold drafts, and tugging people's sleeves. Perhaps she only wants to know how your meal was and to tell you that the flan, they say, is to die for.

Ghost Dogs of Calabasas

In Johnson County, Missouri, on the evening of October 28, 1869, Charles Burden's beloved dog Old Drum was shot and killed by a neighbor. Angered at the cruel manner in which Old Drum was taken from him, the heartbroken Burden sued his neighbor, Leonidas Hornsby, for one hundred dollars in a case that would eventually end up in the Missouri Supreme Court.

In his September 23, 1870, closing remarks Burden's attorney George Graham Vest eloquently spoke of the goodness of dogs.

> The one absolutely unselfish friend that man can have in this selfish world, the one that never deserts him, the one that never proves ungrateful or treacherous is his dog. A man's dog stands by him in prosperity and in poverty, in health and in sickness . . . Gentlemen of the Jury, a man's dog stands by him in prosperity and poverty, in health, and in sickness.

Every dog (pet) owner knows the truth of Vest's words, hence the existence of pet cemeteries. The Los Angeles Pet Memorial Park and Crematorium is the largest pet cemetery on the West Coast. Located in Calabasas, the cemetery was created in 1928 by veterinarian Dr. Eugene Jones; a year later a mortuary and crematory were added. Today there are over forty thousand graves, crypts, and niches within the cemetery.

Some well-known animals rest here at the Los Angeles Pet Memorial Park. Kabar, the beloved pet of silent-screen star Rudolph Valentino, was among the first famous pets to be buried here. According to paranormal writer and ghost expert Richard Senate, Kabar is California's most famous ghost dog. Kabar is also the cemetery resident who receives the most visitors. His apparition has been spotted throughout the cemetery since his death on January 17, 1929. The ghostly dog is said to come when he is called. Even when he chooses not to appear, Kabar has been known to approach fans and lick their hands.

The ghostly canine figures in one of the many legends that surround the actor's death. Kabar was a gift to Valentino and his wife, Natacha Rambova. Valentino fell in love with the Doberman-mix puppy on sight. Kabar reciprocated. We all know how quickly pets can snuggle their way into our hearts. Soon the two were inseparable. And then Valentino needed to go to New York. For some reason he left Kabar at home in Hollywood and traveled off to New York to promote his latest film, *Son of Sheik.*

The two would never see each other again—in this life. While in New York Rudolph Valentino died, leaving fans devastated. It was August 23, 1926, and Kabar was suddenly without his dearest friend. It's been reported that at the moment of Valentino's death Kabar began to howl so loudly that it scared actress Beatrice Lillie. Animals know when something is wrong. As far as Beatrice Lillie goes, it may have been too much bootleg alcohol that caused her automobile mishap mentioned in Kabar's obituary.

Besides the German shepherd movie star Rin-Tin-Tin, Kabar is probably the only dog ever to have had an obituary posted in the newspapers, and it was carried in several.

> The death and burial of Kabar, Rudolph Valentino's favorite dog and companion, recall the sort of dog and man companionship that Senator Vest of Missouri immortalized in his famous speech.
>
> Kabar was a Doberman Pinscher given to Valentino on a trip to Europe while the star was still happily married to Natacha Rambova.
>
> Kabar, only a few months old, was taken to the French estate of the Hudnut family, to which Natacha belonged, and there trained. He was with Valentino constantly, even sleeping in Rudy's chamber at night.
>
> The ill-fated trip to New York that ended in sudden death of the film idol was made without Kabar,

who stayed at home in Falcons Lair, Rudy's mountain home above Hollywood.

It was the loud howls of Kabar at the time of Rudy's death that so frightened Beatrice Lillie that she ran her car off the mountain road and fainted on her way home from a party at Jack Gilbert's house.

With the peculiar intuition credited to dogs, Kabar was aware that something serious was wrong with his master, and his howls with those of the other dogs in the Valentino kennel, could not be quieted.

The arrival of Alberto Guglielmi, brother of Rudolph, allayed the grief somewhat, but the dog has been almost constantly sick since Valentino's death.

Pet cemetery established

The death of Kabar brought up the question of what to do with his remains. In spite of being the center of romantic sentiment and possessed of delightful old traditions and atmosphere since the days when Louise Fazenda's father owned a large stable on the site of the present railway station, Los Angeles has an unsympathetic way of dealing with dead pets.

There is no crematory for animals, and in the past it has been the soap works for all the pampered dogs once dyspepsia caught up with them. Pets were not permitted to be buried except in a cemetery set aside for that purpose under city grant and approval.

The death of Kabar brings to public attention the fact that such a cemetery for dogs of noted lineage has been dedicated near Calabasas in the San Fernando Valley. One hundred thousand dollars was spent on this most lavish of pet cemeteries with landscaping and improvements of various sorts. A chapel, crematory, monumental plant, embalming laboratories, casket shop, day and night hearse service, and other conveniences are part of the plan. Kabar's headstone bears this epitaph:

> Kabar, Rudolph Valentino's Dog
> Born in Alsace June 20, 1922
> Died January 17, 1929

Contrary to the obit, Kabar's actual headstone reads simply:

> Kabar
> My Faithful Dog
> Owner Rudolph Valentino

Split Pea Soup

*M*ost travelers agree. There is no better split pea soup than that found at Pea Soup Andersen's on Highway 33 in Santa Nella and on the Avenue of the Flags in Buellton, the original location. The quest for a hot bowl of soup on a cold day can be satisfied at either location. But the quest for a ghost tale takes us to Pea Soup Andersen's Inn in Buellton just a mile from the restaurant.

It all started when successful dairy farmer R. T. Buell died in 1905 and was buried in the family plot. On that day Buell's family had no idea that progress would one day threaten the family plot. In 1924 electricity was brought to the area and Anton and Juliette Andersen saw opportunity. They bought land along the road and opened a restaurant. The town of Buellton was growing. Four years later the Andersens purchased land that included the Buell family plot. R. T. Buell was disinterred and buried at Oak Hill Cemetery in Solvang, seven miles east.

In 1947 the Andersens changed the name of their café to Pea Soup Andersen's. And this was the beginning of the split pea phenomenon—and the ghostly man. The parking lot of the Pea Soup Andersen's Inn sits upon what was once the Buell family plot. Destroying the sanctity of the grave is never a good idea, although it happens. And when it does, the results can lead to a haunting. For this reason some believe that R. T. Buell is the ghostly man who's been seen in the parking lot of the hotel. Those who've encountered him say he doesn't appear angry at having been relocated—only confused.

Back to the restaurant and the all-you-can-eat split pea soup. The recipe for the famous soup was brought from France by Juliette herself. And it is Juliette who is generally believed to be the ghost in the kitchen. Perhaps she only hangs around to make sure that the soup is being prepared to her ghostly specifications. She is blamed for doors that open and slam close, lights that flicker, and sacré bleu misplaced cooking utensils.

Glen Tavern Inn

In 1873 businessman Nathan Weston Blanchard purchased 2,700 acres and laid out the town site of Santa Paula. Two years later, Blanchard planted the first orange trees in the area. By the time the town of Santa Paula was incorporated in 1902, its main industry was citrus fruit and oil. Nine years later, the film industry discovered Santa Paula when Gaston Méliès brought his Star Films Company from San Antonio, Texas. Soon other filmmakers followed.

In 1911 the Glen Tavern Inn was built across from the train station to serve the train-traveling public. In its heyday celebrities like John Barrymore, Steve McQueen, and Harry Houdini spent time at the Glen Tavern. No one could have guessed that the Glen Tavern's ghosts would be the twenty-first century's tourism impetus. Ghosts are the reason Zak Bagans and the *Ghost Adventures* TV show came to the Glen Tavern, and the reason Amy Allan and Steve DiSchiavi of *The Dead Files* were there as well. Ghosts are also the reason my husband, Bill, and I went.

Actually it was a ghost conference, or ParaCon as we ghost enthusiasts say. And I was one of the speakers. There were a lot of us. Some I knew, some I didn't. Our room was on the third floor next to that of another speaker. Being early risers, Bill and I were up bright and early at seven the first morning—and talking. The walls must have been paper thin. The person in the room next to ours pounded on the wall for silence. We weren't talking loudly; nonetheless we lowered our voices to whispers and thought no more about it.

Fast forward to the next morning, actually 2 a.m. Bill and I were sound asleep. We'd dined with friends, done the ghost hunt, and were sleeping peacefully until a party in the next room woke us. A party? And we hadn't even been invited. Laughter and music and—wait a minute—turnabout is fair play. Bill knocked on the wall for quiet. After his third knock, there was a deathly silence from the room next door. One minute there was laughter and gaiety and the next, nothing.

The next day, I told a friend about the incident. He looked at me baffled. "There was no party. The man who was staying in that room was downstairs with me and we were checking out some new equipment," he said.

"At two o'clock in the morning?" I asked.

He nodded. Here I remembered that not all ghost investigators go to bed early.

"Then who was making all the noise?" I asked.

He shrugged his shoulders. "Probably one of the ghosts."

There are a number of ghostly residents at the Glen Tavern. So which ghost was it? It couldn't have been the ghostly prostitute and a gaggle of her friends. According to legend she was decapitated in one of the rooms to keep her silence. That certainly wouldn't be anything to laugh about.

It wasn't the famous movie dog Rin-Tin-Tin. Although Rinny is said to haunt the Glen Tavern, he certainly wasn't popping the corks off champagne bottles and partying in the next room. Rin-Tin-Tin had his own suite at the Glen Tavern while filming the 1926 silent movie *The Night Cry*. He might have liked the accommodations so much he has stayed on. More than one person has seen the sprightly German shepherd run down the hall only to vanish into thin air. Then, too, there is the barking that isn't that of any living dog.

Perhaps it was the ghostly Calvin, a cheating poker player who was punished for his misdeeds with a bullet. Calvin was involved in an illegal card game on the third floor during Prohibition. He is the most popular ghost at the Glen Tavern. But why would he be having a party? Later I learned that there is indeed a ghostly party that takes place on the third floor of the hotel. Bill and I aren't the only two people to have heard them.

So there it is. The answer to the age-old question—what do people do in the afterlife? They party, especially if they happen to be at the Glen Tavern Inn where ghosts are always welcome.

Kate Morgan and the Hotel Del Coronado

She is buried at Mount Hope Cemetery in San Diego. And with death being the great equalizer that it is, she is not the only person with a connection to the Hotel Del Coronado resting here. Elisha Babcock, builder of the hotel is here. As is Alonzo Horton, the father of San Diego. She reposes at Lot 28, Row 6, Section 1, Division 5. She is Kate Morgan and she is the resident ghost at the Hotel Del Coronado.

The luxurious Hotel Del Coronado was built in 1888 on Coronado Island, approximately twenty miles from downtown San Diego, with an eye toward enticing Southern California's affluent tourists. It certainly worked. Eleven US presidents have stayed at the hotel. If you're curious, they are: Taft, Harrison, Roosevelt, Johnson, Reagan, Ford, Carter, George H. W. Bush, George W. Bush, Clinton, and Obama. Celebrities like Charlie Chaplin, Bette Davis, Kirk Douglas, Gary Cooper, and Lana Turner have stayed here as well.

Movie buffs no doubt know that the 1958 comedy classic *Some Like it Hot*, starring Marilyn Monroe, Tony Curtis, and Jack Lemmon, was filmed here at the Hotel Del Coronado. But it is the ghostly Kate Morgan who continues to draw visitors. According to one legend, the ghostly Kate doesn't like Marilyn Monroe merchandise in the hotel gift shop very much. She is accused of moving Marilyn items around or knocking them down altogether. Kate's been haunting the hotel so long, she may feel that Monroe's image is tawdry or that she is grabbing too much of the spotlight.

Kate Morgan's name became intertwined with that of the Hotel Del Coronado when she died five days after checking in. She came to the hotel alone on Thursday, November 24, 1892. She registered under the name of Mrs. Lottie A. Bernard and was given Room 302. Those who want to stay in the room and attempt to communicate with Kate should be aware that the room has since been renumbered and is now 3327.

During her stay at the hotel, Kate kept to herself spending most of her time in her room. In reporting Kate Morgan's mysterious death, all newspapers had to go on was the alias she used at check in, Lottie A. Bernard. Until her identity was established, newspaper stories referred to her as the Beautiful Stranger. Everything else depends on which legend you care to believe.

November 29, 1892. Kate Morgan's body was discovered in an exterior staircase outside her room. Nearby lay the gun she'd been shot with. Suicide or murder? The coroner determined her death to be a suicide. But why had she done it, this beautiful stranger?

According to those employees who interacted with her during her stay at the Del Coronado, Kate Morgan was a very unhappy and very ill young woman. Then, of course, there was the possibility that she was pregnant and unwed.

Regardless of her reasons for staying on at the Del Coronado indefinitely, the ghostly Kate makes her presence known by turning televisions on and off and sending a cold draft wafting through the room. If that isn't enough to convince a guest of her presence, Kate occasionally appears at the foot of the bed.

Thankfully the Hotel Del Coronado is one haunted hotel that doesn't deny the ghostly stories. The hotel embraces its ghost and even sells books and other mementoes in the gift shop about Kate and her haunting of the hotel. Perhaps this makes the ghostly Kate feel safe and welcome.

Joshua Tree Inn: Gram Parsons and Coffin Flambé

*L*ike unworldly sentinels, Joshua trees stand along the roadways of California's Mojave Desert. Native to the arid Mojave Desert region, these yucca palms might have a lifespan of five hundred years. Still, they are rare, growing only in the Mojave Desert region of California, Nevada, Utah, and Arizona, and only at elevations from two thousand to six thousand feet. No one is certain when these strange-looking plants were first dubbed Joshua trees. Regardless, the name has stuck—so much so that those who live in this region know them as no other name. Just as skyscrapers are synonymous to New York, Joshua trees are synonymous to the Mojave.

Those who live in Los Angeles yearn for smaller, uncrowded places to relax. In their quest, many are lured to the desert, two hours from the city. This is probably the reason that the Joshua Tree Inn was built in 1949. Located approximately forty miles from Joshua Tree National Park, the inn is an ideal spot for getting away from it all.

Among those who fell under the desert's spell was '70s rocker/song-writer Gram Parsons. A native Floridian, Parsons was hooked at first sight. On his way up in the music industry, Parsons kept a tight performance schedule. But this didn't stop him from coming to the Joshua Tree Inn and Joshua Tree National Park whenever he got the chance. It's been reported that he came not only to escape the rigors of his career, but also to do drugs and search the clear night skies for UFOs.

As a regular customer he had a favorite room. That was Room 8, which has since become known as the Gram Parsons Room. This is the room most likely associated with ghostly activity. After all, it is the room in which he spent his last night on earth. As homage to Parsons, the room is kept somewhat as it was during his life. Look in the mirror; this is the same mirror Parsons may have gazed into. The picture on the wall is the very same picture that was here when

133

Parsons checked in. But progress and redecorating have come, so that nothing else of Parsons's time remains. It is believed that the ghost of Gram Parsons stays here in Room 8, remorseful for those last drugged-out days and nights of his life that sent him to an early grave. But then again, here he is, moving small items around and appearing before those he feels are worthy of such an appearance.

Fans from all over the world come to stay in this room where the legend spent his final hours. My late friend Suzie Dwyer was one of them. A true renaissance woman, a woman of eclectic tastes, Suzy was a world traveler who spoke Urdu as well as her native English. An avid paranormal enthusiast and recorder of EVP, she made the drive from Las Vegas to Joshua Tree several times a year. On one particular occasion she brought along a new boyfriend, hoping he would find the area as interesting as she did. He didn't.

The place lacked the excitement of Las Vegas, and he was bored. Soon they were arguing in Room 8. As the night wore on the spat ended and Suzy's boyfriend fell asleep. Unperturbed she took out her voice recorder and tried to communicate with Gram Parsons. She'd always felt he was still here. As she tried to get EVP, warmth pervaded the room. There was nothing to be afraid of. Parsons's spirit was welcoming and kind.

"This isn't going to last. Here we are fighting again," she whispered into her recorder. "He didn't even make love to me tonight."

An hour passed. She let the recorder run on, then snapped it off and went to sleep.

Back in Las Vegas the next night, Suzy turned on the recorder and listened. She smiled when she heard herself saying, "He didn't even make love to me tonight."

She was unprepared for the reply she had recorded. Enough to make most people blush, the words were unmistakable; class A, EVP experts call it. It was a man, but Suzy was convinced the voice was not that of Gram Parsons.

He wouldn't say something so trashy. He wasn't the sort . . . and besides that, he isn't the only person to have spent time in Room 8.

She was right; the voice could be that of anyone who'd occupied the room in the years since Gram Parsons's death on September 19, 1973.

Parsons's life began winding down the moment he unlocked the door and stepped into Room 8. His heavy drug and alcohol use was finally about to catch up with him. He had come to his beloved desert, as he always did, for a little R and R before going on tour. A little R and R and a lotta drugs; Parsons and his pals would party hardy. So hardy, in fact, that two days after checking into the motel, twenty-five-year-old Gram Parsons slipped out of this world.

While his family made arrangements to have the body shipped to New Orleans for burial, distraught friends were left to mourn Gram and his final wishes that his family wasn't honoring. Something had to be done. Parsons's pals knew that he wanted to be cremated and his ashes scattered across Cap Rock at Joshua Tree National Park. Two of them made a bold plan. They borrowed an old black hearse and went to the Los Angeles International Airport as Parsons's coffin was being readied for transport.

They told attendants that the family had changed its mind. They now wanted the body flown from the Van Nuys Municipal Airport. No questions were asked; the coffin bearing the deceased Parsons was loaded into the hearse, and they sped toward the desert. When they reached Joshua Tree National Park, they opened the coffin and poured in five gallons of gasoline. A match was lit and the cremation was underway. The resulting fireball could be seen a mile away.

Days later the two men were arrested. But there were no laws on the books at that time regarding the stealing of bodies. And so, they were merely fined for stealing the coffin. They had helped their friend the best they could.

Today that spot in Joshua Tree National Park is seen by fans as an unofficial memorial to Gram Parsons. Occasionally a ranger may point out the spot to curious fans. Otherwise there is no mention here of Gram Parsons. Still, there are ghost investigators who believe that Parsons returns to this area on the anniversary of his strange cremation—just to check things out.

He'd done duets with Emmylou Harris, and performed with the Byrds, the Flying Burrito Brothers, and the International Submarine Band. If not for the deadly combination of morphine and alcohol, Gram Parsons may have reached the pinnacle of success in country music. And he might still be coming to spend time in Room 8 at the Joshua Tree Inn on Twenty-nine Palms Highway. But then again, there are those who say that he still does.

Ganna and the Ghost Who
Changed His Mind

*H*er dream was to become a world-renowned opera star. While that dream went unfulfilled, she is not forgotten. Rather than being remembered for her beauty and her voice, Ganna Walska is remembered for the exquisite botanical garden she helped to create at Lotusland. This is her legacy; a testament to her remarkable eye for beauty. Those visiting the thirty-seven-acre Lotusland, located in Montecito, may find it difficult to find a ghostly connection to this tranquil place where butterflies flitter from one plant to the next and sunshine turns pond water silver. And yet, the eccentric woman who is responsible for all of this came to California on the advice of her last husband, a yogi, who wanted the garden to be called Tibetland, a refuge for Tibetan monks.

Can you imagine taking dating advice from an ex who happens to also be a ghost? Ganna did. Hanna (Ganna) Puacz's life began in 1887 in Brest-Litovsk, Poland, during the reign of Alexander III. While studying in Russia the nineteen-year-old beauty caught the eye of Baron Arcadie d'Eingorn, an officer in Czar Nicholas II's army. After a brief courtship the baron proposed and Hanna eagerly became his wife.

But the marriage was not what she'd imagined in her romantic fantasies. Her husband was a philanderer and an abusive drunk. Vowing never again to make a similar matrimonial mistake, she wasted no time in divorcing the errant baron. Somewhere around this time Hanna Puacz changed her name to the darkly mysterious Madame Ganna (the Russian version of Hanna) Walska, an opera singer, even though she couldn't sing a note.

Nonetheless the idea of being an international opera star appealed to Ganna. She packed what she could carry and left Russia, sailing for New York in 1918. Matchmaking friends introduced her to Dr. Julius Fraenkel, the famed New York endocrinologist. Like the baron before him, Fraenkel was captivated by Ganna's beauty. The thirty-year age difference between Ganna and Dr. Fraenkel didn't bother either one of them. The romance was a whirlwind. They were married months after their first meeting. This time Ganna had chosen wisely. Her venture into matrimony would prove successful emotionally and financially. The happy couple were married only two years when Dr. Fraenkel died unexpectedly, leaving his entire estate of $350,000 dollars to his young widow. That may sound paltry until you consider that the $350,000 of 1920 is roughly equivalent to $8 million today.

Heartbroken, the wealthy and newly widowed Ganna returned to Europe. Aboard ship she encountered two intriguing men: husband number three, Alexander Smith Cochran, and husband number four, Harold Fowler McCormick. The two old friends were charmed by the beguiling Ganna and made a wager on which of them would meet, and date, her first. Cochran won the bet. But McCormick was smitten. When he got back to his Chicago home, he publicly announced that he and his wife were no longer living together, and would soon divorce.

Meanwhile Ganna had begun dating Cochran. And like she had done since his untimely death, she consulted Dr. Fraenkel for advice from the spirit realm. The good doctor was impressed with tycoon Cochran's prospects. And what prospects they were. Cochran was the wealthiest bachelor in the United States. During one of their regular after-death tête-à-têtes the ghostly Dr. Fraenkel offered some invaluable matrimonial guidance to his young widow.

"You must marry Mr. Cochran," he urged. Ganna hesitated. In life Dr. Fraenkel had been a wise doctor; surely in death he still knew best. And so she agreed to become Mrs. Alexander Cochran. Financially, Ganna was now set for life; all her dreams were coming to fruition. The ghostly Dr. Fraenkel should have been elated. He wasn't.

It seemed he had made a terrible mistake. Ganna was never meant to marry Alexander Cochran after all. He urged her to divorce Cochran immediately. She may have ignored the ghostly advice, but things were not so blissful in Cochran's exclusive Murray Hill home. The newlyweds argued too often. Perhaps Dr. Fraenkel was right. So once again, trusting the advice of her ghostly second husband, Ganna hired an attorney. Cochran already had one. The battle began. "If he wants to get rid of me he must pay until it hurts for his own good," Ganna said petulantly.

The wealthy Cochran capitulated: Ganna's divorce settlement was $300,000, traveling money. Ganna packed up and headed for Havana. McCormick was still smitten. When he heard her singing in Cuba, he invited her to come back and star in the Chicago Grand Opera.

The trouble was, Ganna couldn't sing. If not for the fact that McCormick was the opera's financial backer, she would not have been offered the lead role in *Zaza*. Everyone knew it but McCormick himself. He was too blinded by love. The director was not. Ganna could take a hint. Off to Paris she went. McCormick followed.

Gossips were kept busy with the realization that the much older and still married Harold McCormick was also in Paris. And while the divorce attorneys conferenced with their clients in the City of Lights, the discarded spouse sought legal advice back in the United States. Shedding a spouse of thirty-some years would make for an expensive exit. It mattered little to McCormick. He would have Ganna at all costs.

For her part Ganna was still angry at the ghost of Dr. Fraenkel and called him a liar. While she had always believed in the supernatural, she would no longer seek his advice in matters of the heart. Why should she? She was soon to be the wife of Harold McCormick

After the Paris wedding, McCormick hurried back to Chicago. Ganna preferred Paris, and stayed. This was not to be the happily-ever-after marriage she had dreamed of as a young girl. After nine years of a marriage that was conducted from different parts of the world, McCormick divorced her on grounds of desertion.

She would wed six times in her lifetime. Whether or not Dr. Fraenkel approved or disapproved of her next three spouses is anybody's guess. While she continued to attend séances and consult the Ouija board, she did not share information about any further conversations with the ghost of Dr. Fraenkel in her autobiography, *There's Always Room at the Top*.

A Subpoena for Sho Sha

*A*divorce is bad enough. When it involves a ghost as part of the love triangle it's even worse. The 1940 divorce of Dr. and Mrs. William Boyce was on the front pages of newspapers across the country because it involved a ghost.

Although both parties might agree to an amicable split, divorce seldom comes without some soul searching. A marriage failed, dreams of a happily-ever-after dashed—painful stuff, even when the next spouse is waiting in the matrimonial wings.

Summer had barely come to the city. Los Angelinos were already suffering under the intense heat that swept in from the Mojave Desert on dry Santa Ana winds. Lillian Boyce hardly noticed. She had more important things on her mind.

After twenty-two years of marriage, the attractive fifty-six-year-old matron was set to divorce her husband, Dr. William Boyce. There had been some good times. But over the years, they had drifted apart. So far apart that Lillian wondered if there was another woman in the doctor's life. She had her suspicions from the moment she heard him whispering endearments into the telephone. Who was the person he called "darling"?

The Boyces had not been blessed with children. Well-meaning friends were quick to point to this as a godsend when confronting the ugly realities of divorce. Still, there were John, Jane, and Bill, the couple's adored dogs, and they were like children. As any good mother might, Lillian wanted custody of the canines. The dogs needed her. And they loved her. That was more than she could say for her husband.

Where had all the affection gone? Straight to the woman he whispered to on the telephone. Nowadays, he was usually so preoccupied that he hardly paid Lillian any attention. And Lillian was not one to be ignored. She might have been able to overlook it, to find her own hobbies and interests, if not for her husband's objectionable habits. And he had plenty. In her divorce complaint she had listed no less than twenty-five.

Rather than eat his soup quietly as others did, Dr. Boyce slurped his bowl empty. This lack of grace and good manner grated on Lillian's nerves. She often wondered if it wasn't intentional. As if that wasn't enough to toss propriety and good manners aside, the doctor thought nothing of taking his false teeth out in front of others. Disgusting! And a humiliation for Lillian who deeply cared what others thought. Her husband's lack of etiquette was further demonstrated by the fact that he spit tobacco anytime he needed to do so. It didn't matter where he happened to be.

Among the doctor's most abhorrent habits was his very recent and very lurid interest in nudists. Lillian would never understand it. She wouldn't even try. Men and women who chose to run around in the desert without a stitch of clothing on were foolish, not the sort of people she wanted in her life.

Yes, she had plenty of good reasons for calling it quits. Dr. Boyce saw things differently. He had been a good husband. If the marriage was over, it was through no fault of his. The wealthy Hollywood eye specialist filed a countersuit charging Lillian's affections had strayed to the darkly handsome Sheland Shaimond, otherwise known as Sho Sha. But Sho Sha was no ordinary rival. Nor was he just a gigolo seeking to have his good times financed. Sho Sha was a ghost Lillian had met during one of the séances she attended. According to Dr. Boyce, his wife admitted to having fallen in love with the ghostly Sho Sha. So ghost or not, Sheland Shaimond aka Sho Sha was dutifully named as co-respondent in the divorce case. How does one compete with a honey from the hereafter?

The Boyces' day in court came on Friday, July 25. Dr. Boyce was sworn in. The first question asked to him was, "You have named a ghost as co-respondent here?"

"Yes," the doctor calmly answered, "a ghost is an actual co-respondent, which we will prove very conclusively."

Mrs. Boyce's attorney, S. Hahn, was on his feet asking Judge Nye to issue a subpoena ordering the ghostly Sho Sha to appear in court and give testimony.

"Every effort will be made to get him to testify and if necessary to establish the proper séance conditions, we will ask for a night court session. We will bring a medium into court to act as interpreter. . . . If the process servers cannot locate Sho Sha and serve him we are prepared to hold a trumpet séance and call upon him," Hahn assured the judge. He also assured the court that when the ghostly gigolo appeared, his testimony would be taken by slate writing. After some consideration Judge Clement Nye tried to do what Hamlet could not. He issued the subpoena and ordered Sho Sha to appear in court. Since Sho Sha had made his only recorded appearance in Los Angeles County, the subpoena was domestic rather than foreign. It read: For failure to attend you will be deemed guilty of contempt of court and liable to pay damages sustained by the parties aggrieved and forfeit one hundred dollars in addition.

The deputies were stunned. How, they wondered as they accepted the papers, was anyone going to locate the ghostly Sho Sha, much less serve him? Thankfully it wasn't their problem. The job of locating Sho Sha went to process server Max Groman. With papers in hand, Groman went on his ghost hunt. But after a month spent at Forest Lawn, Glendale, and all other area cemeteries, haunted houses, and séance parties, Groman could not find the elusive Sho Sha. In desperation, the process server stopped at Santa Anita racetrack where a disembodied voice told him to place a two-dollar bet on a horse named Spiritualist in the second race. Feeling certain that he had at last located Sho Sha, Groman did as he was told, and waited. But the horse lost and still the ghost made no appearance. Groman returned to court empty-handed, save for the five-hundred-dollar bill for his expenses.

So Sho Sha was a no-show. And the trial went forward without his testimony. Dr. Boyce testified that the ghost and his wife had become close after meeting each other at a séance conducted by Madame Loretta Julian. The elderly Madame Julian was able to make trumpets fly through the air and it was in the trumpets that the voices of the dearly departed were heard.

While he shared his wife's interest in the occult for a time, Dr. Boyce told the court that his enthusiasm waned when he started to question the voices in the trumpet.

"Did you hear those voices in the trumpet?" he was asked.

"I heard whispers; I could not tell where they came from."

"But when those voices came from the trumpet you heard them?"

"Yes and I could smell human breath and have mentioned this to Mrs. Boyce."

"What do you mean by human breath?"

"Did you ever smell bad breath?" the doctor asked.

"Describe it."

"When the trumpet would get up close to my face I have smelt a bad odor as if from a human breath."

He testified that he had asked Mrs. Loretta Julian if there was an epidemic of halitosis in the spirit world. She seemed to take the question as a personal affront and this led him to suspect that the whole thing was a fake. But the ghostly Sho Sha was real and he was trying to destroy the Boyces' marriage.

"She was too fond of him. She said he was very dark and handsome and even thought she saw him one time in a booth at the Mt. Shasta Inn. I wanted to see him too so we went back, but Sho Sha was gone. I finally told her that I was through with spiritualism. I told her I was through with any force that had caused the disharmony it had caused in our family. And about her soul mate; his coming and breaking up our home was a very pernicious thing."

The doctor also testified about the Boyces' past lives. Inevitably the medium found that Lillian had led lives of intrigue and glamour; she had been a beautiful princess in one life and a dancing girl in another. At her side had been the mysterious and darkly handsome Sho Sha. But in his previous incarnations, Dr. Boyce was always ordinary. His earliest past life had been that of Immulus, a lowly captain in the Roman legion.

Mrs. Boyce awaited her day in court.

"In all these episodes I was made always to be wrong and somebody else was the hero," he said.

It must have been especially bitter for the man who was paying for the medium's services. Apparently, the spirits were listening. At the next séance the spirit of Adina, a beautiful maiden he had loved two thousand years ago, came forward. She still longed for him and wanted to travel eternity with him just as Mrs. Boyce and Sho Sha were doing. Nothing doing; Dr. Boyce didn't remember Adina and didn't want to travel eternity with her. The well-timed appearance of Adina roused his suspicions. And he began to investigate. In a novel titled *A Prince in the House of David*, Dr. Boyce discovered characters named Adina and Immulus.

Dr. Boyce's attorney then asked him to read from a letter he had written to his nephew.

"Can we communicate with those gone on? Yes, under certain conditions, through people we call mediums, who are people that are sensitive and can pick up, as it were, the wave lengths that come from the other side. Please understand that a medium is born and knows no more how she has the power than you or I."

Dr. Boyce looked up a moment and continued reading. "Some things I have found out; we all have a beginning but never an ending, as nothing is destroyed, especially human soul. We must live on through eternity. You and I and all the rest have lived many times before."

It was the very thought of his beloved Lillian and her so-called soul mate Sho Sha romping their way through all eternity that rankled.

Finally, it was Mrs. Boyce's turn to take the stand. Her hair stylishly coiffed, and dressed in an elegant suit and matching hat, she took the stand.

In a soft, but determined voice, Lillian explained that it was nothing but jealousy of her exciting previous lives that brought about her husband's denial of the supernatural. Sho Sha was one of many spirits that she regularly conversed with; in fact, George Washington, Jean Harlow, and Will Rogers were among the dearly departed who regularly lifted the veil to speak with her.

Sho Sha, she pointed out, was a teacher, and if her husband didn't understand that it was no one's fault but his own. He didn't vibrate on as high a plane as she did. "Maybe if he didn't drink so much he would," she suggested.

Then she told the court about her husband's interest in nudism.

"We were staying in the desert near Palm Springs where Dr. Boyce met some people who were nudists. He became very interested and wanted us to become nudists. He thought he would try the idea out for a while and went up to the hills wearing only his shorts. He later told me he had an embarrassing time because he had lost his shorts and did not know how he was going to get back without them."

On cross examination she was asked to read a passage from her diary. She calmly stared at the page a moment and read. "Bill and I went to Mrs. Julian's and sat in concentration. Sho Sha laid his hands on my head in such a comforting way."

When asked if she planned on being reunited with Sho Sha after death, Mrs. Boyce testified, "I have no such plans. . . . But I think that would be a beautiful idea. Especially for widows, don't you?"

Much as they do today, the news media sought out experts in the field to explain Mrs. Boyce's fascination with the ghostly Sho Sha.

According to Hereward Carrington, director of the American Psychical Institute, and John Mulholland, magician, author, and paranormal investigator, Sho Sha was an old-fashioned ghost. Not at all what one would expect in the modern 1940s. Carrington said, "The technique of séances has changed almost completely since the early days. Physical manifestations are no longer the rule. Instead the present-day medium likes to go into a trance during which she hears voices that are inaudible to the sitters . . ."

Mulholland, author of *Beware Familiar Spirits,* said, "The séance room which is dark and hushed and very intimate sometimes inspires a feeling of, shall we say, affection, in the sitters, particularly the women. Women are more sensitive to darkness than men are . . . it's not surprising nor so rare, either that women occasionally do fall in love with spirits."

He then went on to say that if Sho Sha had placed his hands upon Mrs. Boyce he was acting against the California Mediums' Association. He explained, "There were too many frauds and deceptions. It got to the point where sometimes even the believers couldn't go on believing any longer. The entire profession was in danger of being discredited. So the California Mediums placed a ban on physical phenomena and shifted the emphasis to mental manifestations from the spirit world."

Two months after it began, Boyce vs. Boyce was concluded on September 25, 1940. Judge Clement D. Nye denied both parties a divorce on insufficient grounds. After awarding Lillian $350 per month as separate maintenance, the judge said:

> She charges that he called her crazy for beliefs and became indifferent, and he replied that Sho Sha had stolen love. Sho Sha was a departed spirit to which his wife was introduced through the agency of a spiritual medium. He remained a voice which came out of a trumpet and was supposed to have been her lover in a previous life, with whom she would be reunited as a soul mate on leaving the earth. As a result Dr. Boyce contends his wife became a changed woman with Sho Sha the dominant and sole interest in her life.
>
> It is without the province of the court to determine whether the parties were justified in their beliefs in the occult.

Strange that neither of the Boyces crossed the California-Nevada border to wait out a six-week divorce residency in Las Vegas, but they didn't. And the litigation continued. It would take two years and thousands of dollars in legal fees, and in the end Dr. Boyce would prevail. On July 31, 1942, after Lillian stopped contesting his suit, he was awarded a divorce from her on the grounds of mental cruelty.

Gaviota Pass

*T*ragedy scars everything. Even the land it happens upon. Originally part of El Camino Real (the King's Highway) that Father Junipero Serra and other padres traversed as they made their way from one mission to the next, Gaviota Pass in the Santa Ynez Mountains is no exception.

According to legend, the name Gaviota (which means seagull in Spanish) was given to this area because conquistadors killed a seagull nearby and named the area after the unfortunate bird. But there is a darker legend here that involves slaughter of Native Americans at Gaviota Pass by Spanish conquistadors. The killings gave rise to ghostly Native Americans who wander the pass, especially on foggy or windy nights.

These were Spanish soldiers who were used to the conquest of whatever, or whoever stood in their way. When they were set upon by native warriors and forced to retreat, the soldiers became angry at the thought of being overcome by natives who they considered to be untrained. In retaliation, they set a fire that quickly engulfed and trapped the warriors who perished in the windswept flames. It's said that on certain nights the ghosts of these men who died in the long ago fire, appear and cry out for justice.

A memorial at Gaviota Pass on Highway 101 commemorates the fact that Captain John Fremont captured Santa Barbara without bloodshed. The Fremont Foxen memorial states that on Christmas 1846 Fremont was set to cross Gaviota Pass. Unbeknownst to Fremont, natives and Spanish soldiers waited in the mountain pass, ready to ambush him and his men. When Benjamin Foxen and his son William learned of the plot they warned Fremont to take a different route. He did so and thus he averted bloodshed. Some historians argue this incident didn't happen. And that may well be. Regardless, Gaviota Pass is a scenic area of Santa Barbara County, ghosts or not.

Pasadena Playhouse

*E*very theater is probably haunted. Think about it. What actor wants to leave the stage, much less the theater? Certainly not Pasadena Playhouse founder Gilmor Brown. When he founded the Pasadena Playhouse in 1917 Gilmor Brown had a vision of what it could be and worked tirelessly to bring that dream to fruition. The playhouse's popularity led to its 1937 designation by the California state legislature as the Official State Theater of California. That same year the school of theater arts that Brown had added to the playhouse became an accredited college. Its students included TV's Perry Mason, Raymond Burr, and TV's Superman, George Reeves. Obviously, they were paying attention in class. Other alumni of the playhouse include such notables as Dustin Hoffman, Leonard Nimoy, Sally Struthers, and Ruth Buzzi.

The eccentric Gilmor Brown was a perfectionist who watched rehearsals with his cat. If the cat turned its back to the players, Brown insisted the scene be re-done until the cat turned back around. Apparently, the feline was that good of a theater critic. Dead over sixty years, the ghostly Gilmor Brown and his cat haunt the playhouse to this day, just to make sure everything is as it should be. It's said that Gilmor is a practical joke–playing ghost. He moves things around, turns the lights on and off, and can sometimes be heard stomping through the theater. A word of caution: He gets irritated when someone sits at his desk in the VIP room.

This is when he noisily shuffles props, and if you listen you will hear the cat shrieking. Gilmor and his cat don't want for ethereal company. They are not the only ghostly inhabitants. A costumed actress has been seen in the green room by several actors. A man tried to make conversation with her only to have her smile, turn, and walk right through the wall. Several ghost investigators have investigated the Pasadena Playhouse and concur with those who've seen or heard something unworldly—the place is haunted. But isn't every theater?

Pasadena's Haunted Suicide Bridge

*T*he Colorado Boulevard Bridge, which spans the Arroyo Seco, has been known locally as the Suicide Bridge for many years. It's located a little over a mile from Pasadena's famous Rose Bowl. Both are historic landmarks with very different auras. Where people come to the Rose Bowl to cheer on their favorite college football team, or grab a bargain at the world-famous Rose Bowl Flea Market, people visit the bridge for very different reasons.

Legend has it that the ghost of a worker who fell to his death during construction hangs around the bridge coaxing people to jump and join him in the afterlife. He is not the only ghost at the bridge. Many of those who died here still wander the bridge or the area below it in the Arroyo Seco. There is also the ghost of a big yellow dog who's been seen wandering the bridge in the predawn hours.

When the bridge was completed in 1913, people had already started to leap to their death from it. By 1935, sixty-five people had chosen to end it all here. After a sixteen-year-old school girl, despondent over a bad grade, jumped to her death, the Pasadena city board was faced with trying to find a way to prevent suicide. No matter what ideas they tried, the suicides continued.

But then, so did a wedding. At midnight on Friday the 13th (December 13), Officer Joseph F. Willis and Ethel McVey were married by Reverend J. H. Price, who pronounced them man and wife on the bridge. While some people might shy away from having their wedding performed on Suicide Bridge on Friday the 13th, the bride and groom certainly didn't.

With the Reverend J. H. Price and their families looking on, the happy couple gushed to the newspaper writer, "We're not superstitious."

Maybe they should have been. Five years later they were divorced.

On May 1, 1937, Mrs. Myrtle Ward saw her life as hopeless. Her husband had left her; she didn't know how she was going to take care of herself and her three-year-old daughter. She parked near the bridge, walked up to the edge, and tossed her daughter over. And then she jumped. By some miracle, the little girl's life was saved when she landed in trees and bushes. Much later in life, she would say that angels had saved her life on that sunny morning in 1937.

Myrtle Wood's ghost is one of the ghosts who are said to wander the bridge. Wearing a long, shimmering white dress, the ghostly Myrtle cries out for her daughter. Over the years several motorists have encountered the sorrowful specter.

Since its construction, more than 150 people have chosen to commit suicide from the bridge. All these deaths have lent a dark aura to the bridge. As part of a twenty-seven-million-dollar renovation in 1993 a concrete barrier was erected, and although it has cut down on the number of suicides, people still manage to find a way to end their lives here.

Chief Buffalo Child Long Lance and Lucky Baldwin

Chief Buffalo Child Long Lance aka Sylvester Clark Long must be the rudest guest anyone has ever admitted to their home. On March 20, 1932, while visiting at the luxurious home of Lucky Baldwin, Long Lance, a former security guard for the family, decided to commit suicide. Imagine the Baldwins' dismay. Imagine Long Lance's when he realized that he would be haunting the Baldwin estate forever.

During the late 1920s Long Lance was well known and in demand as a speaker. This was because of his well-received 1928 autobiography that talked about growing up as the son of a Blackfoot chief in Montana. His starring role in the 1929 film titled *The Silent Enemy* attempted to accurately depict life as a Native American and increased his celebrity. But, sadly, Long Lance was living a lie. He wasn't born anywhere near Montana, but in Winston-Salem, North Carolina, in 1890. His real name was Sylvester Clark Long and both his parents were former slaves. When the truth came to light, his career was destroyed and most of his friends deserted him. He started drinking heavily. Then came the night in March 1932 when forty-one-year-old Long Lance ended it all. Or did he?

Since his death, witnesses have claimed to see Long Lance walking the grounds. Some have even reportedly carried on conversations with the ghostly Long Lance.

The former Baldwin estate is located within the 127-acre Los Angeles Arboretum in Arcadia. If you've ever watched an episode of the popular 1977–1984 TV drama *Fantasy Island*, you've seen the Baldwin mansion. When Tattoo (played by Hervé Villechaize) comes out of Mr. Roark's (played by Ricardo Montalbán) home calling "Ze Plane! Ze plane!", he is actually coming out the front door of the Baldwin mansion at the arboretum.

It's said that several members of the film crew encountered the ghostly Long Lance during the filming of *Fantasy Island.* He is not the only ghost on the grounds. The arboretum, especially the Queen Anne Cottage, is also said to be haunted by Lucky Baldwin and one of his four wives. The question is which wife is Baldwin's companion in the hereafter?

Maybe they all are there with Lucky. This would explain the noisy bickering that's been reported by some visitors to the arboretum.

A Smiling Ghost

*H*ard to believe, but the story of a smiling ghost appeared in the January 30, 1947, issue of the *Gasconade Republican*. In Los Angeles two frightened women called the police for protection from a smiling ghost. Mrs. Viola Jaggers and her sister-in-law Edith were frantic for the nightly haunting to stop.

They explained that Viola's dog, Spotty, was also petrified of the ghostly visitor who appeared in the window at 9:25 p.m. every night, and smiled as the lights flashed on and off and the sickly strong aroma of gardenias wafted through the air. This, they said, even though there were no gardenia plants in the neighborhood.

Mrs. Jaggers said that in the four years she'd lived there, something strange went on nearly every night. Mrs. Jaggers admitted she hadn't believed her sister-in-law about the haunted bedroom until she saw it for herself.

"I decided to prove once and for all there was nothing to Edith's hallucinations, so I went to the room, shut the door, and turned off the lights. In a few minutes the window was lit up by a soft light—like moonlight. Then I saw the face of a big man looking at me. He smiled, but didn't speak. I ran from the room and got my husband, Frank. We turned off the light and in a moment or so we saw another face at the window. In the face there were holes where eyes should have been. It was the face of a dead man."

There was no word on where exactly the haunted home was, what the police discovered, or whether or not the jittery Jaggers moved from their haunted abode.

Zane Grey Estate

*A*lthough it is private property, the Zane Grey Estate in Altadena was placed on the National Register of Historic Places in 2002 because of its connection to famed Western writer Zane Grey. The 7,240-square-foot house was built in 1907 and purchased by Zane Grey and his wife in 1920. Under the Greys' ownership a third-floor addition and a two-story east wing were added to the house in 1928.

Many of Grey's books were written at the home, even though he had a secluded cabin, traveled extensively, and wrote at other locations. Zane Grey died suddenly at his Altadena home on October 23, 1939. He was sixty-seven years old. Do writers really ever stop writing? Rumor has it that the author still wanders his Western-style mansion. There are reports of phantom footsteps and cold spots throughout the mansion. Cold spots are a dead giveaway, no pun intended, that there is paranormal activity afoot. But is it the writer himself, or just some other ghost who happens to like the house?

So far, the ghostly Zane Grey has not made an appearance. If he is in residence, Grey may soon have new housemates. At this writing, the estate is currently on the market for close to four million dollars.

Hueneme, the Lady of Mugu Rock

On January 31, 2000, Alaska Airlines flight 261 took off from Licenciado Gustavo Diaz Ordaz International Airport in Puerto Vallarta, Jalisco, Mexico, with eighty-eight people on board. The plane was en route to San Francisco and was more than halfway there when something went wrong with the aircraft. An emergency landing at LAX (Los Angeles International Airport) was requested and approved.

While pilots communicated with the tower, the problem the plane was experiencing went from bad to worse. During the last eleven minutes of the flight, the captain and the first officer tried desperately to gain control of the plane and right a jammed stabilizer. At 4:22 p.m. the plane nosedived into 650-foot-deep ocean waters, south of Point Mugu. All eighty-eight people on board were killed. This tragedy is well documented, and probably best known locally, but it is not the only tragedy to have occurred in this area.

Hueneme's beautiful glowing ghost is sometimes seen at Mugu Rock where she chose to kill herself rather than lose the love of her life. According to an ancient local legend, Hueneme was a beautiful Chumash princess who fell in love with, and married, an equally handsome young man. Their happiness gave rise to the jealousy of another young woman who loved Hueneme's husband from afar. When she couldn't steal him from Hueneme, she turned to a local witch to teach her the witchcraft skills that would cause him to abandon Hueneme and fall in love with her.

Under the other woman's spell, he rejected Hueneme and went to the other woman. Heartbroken, Hueneme begged him to return to her. But bedazzled, he refused. There was nothing for Hueneme to do but walk out into the waters at Mugu Rock. And there she was swept out to the ocean depths. Filled with despair, her husband came to his senses and chose to join his wife in death. It is said that Hueneme was turned into Mugu Rock and her husband became a nearby rock so that they are together to eternity.

There have been numerous violent, accidental deaths and suicides here at Mugu Rock. Some say this is a result of the evil woman who stole Hueneme's husband long ago. The ghostly Hueneme never says a word; she merely wanders the area around Mugu Rock as if searching for something.

Santa Monica Pier and Carousel

If ghosts just want to have fun, as some believe, what better place to do so than an amusement park? Apparently, some specters have chosen to enjoy themselves at the Santa Monica Pier carousel. A ghostly man is often spotted riding one horse or another on the carousel that dates back to the early 1900s.

In 1916 Charles Loof and his son Arthur built the Newcomb Pier, adjacent to the Santa Monica Pier, to accommodate Loof's carousel, which was housed in a large hippodrome. And here is where the ghostly action occurs. The carousel is sometimes switched on long after the pier has closed for the day. This is when they come out. And there is some question as to who these people who seem to be enjoying the amusement park are. Those who've witnessed the ghostly crowd say they aren't walking so much as floating just above the pier. But don't think that ghostly occurrences happen only after dark. A man claimed to be tapped on the shoulder in broad daylight by a woman who smiled at him as if she knew him, then turned and vanished back into the hippodrome.

The amusement park at the pier is iconic and has been featured in numerous TV shows, movies, and music videos over the years. Perhaps a ghost even managed to appear as an extra in a crowd scene. Stranger things have happened.

George Woolf's at the Derby

*I*n 2011 the Arcadia Historical Society placed a History Lives Here marker at the Derby. And indeed, it does. The Derby has been around forever—for the better part of a century, anyway. The Derby is a classy little place on Arcadia's Huntington Drive—and it's haunted by an early owner, George Woolf. Known as the Iceman for his cool and calm before a big race, Jockey Woolf made a nice bit of cash riding Seabiscuit to victory against the favored War Admiral in the 1938 Pimlico Special at Baltimore. That same year Woolf and his wife, Genevieve, purchased the Derby in Arcadia.

Located a little over a mile from the Santa Anita Park racetrack, the Derby was the perfect place for race fans. At the helm was the Iceman himself. And he added to the racetrack allure by decorating the walls of the eatery with racing memorabilia and photographs. Soon the Derby was a popular Arcadia dining spot. This suited the eccentric Woolf who wore custom cowboy boots and sported several rings. He embraced his fame and liked nothing better than holding court at a favorite barstool, greeting his patrons warmly, and swapping horse race tales.

Sadly, George Woolf's death came early and swiftly. It happened on the afternoon of January 3, 1946, during the fourth race at Santa Anita. Woolf was riding Please Me when he suddenly fell from the horse, striking his head on the ground. He died of a brain concussion at St. Luke's Hospital in Pasadena the next day. He was four months shy of his thirty-sixth birthday.

The horse racing world was shocked. Notables gathered to pay homage and cowboy movie star/singer Gene Autry sang "Empty Saddles" at his funeral. After a period of mourning Genevieve Woolf continued to run the Derby. In 1950 Santa Anita Park began awarding the George Woolf Memorial Jockey Award. The award is presented annually to the thoroughbred horse racing jockey in North

America who demonstrates high professional and personal standards. The winner is chosen by his or her peers. The award is a foot-tall replica of the life-size statue of George Woolf that was erected in the Paddock Gardens at Santa Anita Park. And thus, George Woolf, the Iceman, is honored.

In 1952 Genevieve sold the Derby, giving the new owners scrapbooks she'd kept, some of George's whips, and even the silks he was wearing on that fateful January day in 1946. These items and other racing memorabilia are on display at the Derby.

Not on display, but active nonetheless, is George the Iceman, Woolf's ghost. And he's said to prefer the barstool at the same spot he liked in life. Some say they can actually feel his presence. And those who've worked in the empty restaurant after hours have told of hearing footsteps and of straightening the stools only to return the next day to find that one stool has been turned at an odd angle away from the others.

Death Valley Ghosts

*T*here's something about the name Death Valley that conjures up a lot of very unpleasant thoughts. Some of the highest land temperatures ever recorded take place in the 3,000-square-mile Death Valley that sits in the Mojave Desert. Don't go out and about here without a couple of canteens full of water. Those who didn't have enough water perished. Some men perished in other ways. Such is the case of Joe Simpson. Lest you go thinking that Joe was an innocent, he wasn't. Joe was the local bad hombre of a mining town in Death Valley called Skidoo.

Joe had a short temper that flourished after too many shots of whiskey. On April 19, 1908, Joe got drunk and shot Jim Arnold, one of Skidoo's leading citizens. Jim was taken to the undertakers and Joe was taken to jail to await trial. Unfortunately, this didn't work out very well for Joe. On April 22, 1908, a group of angry vigilantes came calling for Joe at the jail with a rope. Legend has it that Joe died of a heart attack as he was being led to a makeshift scaffold. Alive or dead, Joe was lynched.

That was certainly an indignity, but not the worst that Joe Simpson was subjected to. After being declared dead, Joe's body was taken down by Dr. McDonald and an autopsy was performed. Then Dr. McDonald cut off Joe's head and opened it up for observation. Apparently, Joe suffered from syphilis and the good doctor was studying its effects on the body. Once he was done with his study, Dr. McDonald boiled the head until all the flesh fell off. The skull was kept by Dr. McDonald as a souvenir of his time in Skidoo. It's anyone's guess where the rest of Joe's body went.

The ghost town of Skidoo is located in Death Valley National Park, which happens to be the largest national park in the contiguous US. Time has moved on. And there's not much left of Skidoo today—nothing except for the angry, headless ghost of Joe Simpson who wanders the area in search of his head.

An hour and a half up the road is the Furnace Creek Inn. Established in 1927 by the Pacific Coast Borax Company, the inn was soon expanded from twelve rooms to sixty-six and became a getaway destination for the likes of Bette Davis, William Powell, and countless other celebrities. Clark Gable and his bride Carole Lombard spent their honeymoon at Furnace Creek Inn after marrying in Kingman, Arizona. Apparently, none of these stars decided to spend eternity here at Furnace Creek Inn. It's probably too hot. But there are those ghosts who can stand the heat in the kitchen and the desert.

The ghost at the Furnace Creek Inn is a chef who worked here for over twenty years. He loved his job, but illness forced him to retire. Brokenhearted, the chef left Death Valley and died a few years later. And that's when weird things started happening in the kitchen. Have you ever seen a spoon fly through the air? If you worked in the kitchen you might have. Equipment was moved or disappeared altogether. And kitchen staff kept bumping into the late chef. Occasionally he even wandered out into the dining areas, toque blanche and all.

But there is a solution to every problem. The kitchen was remodeled, and everything rearranged in an effort to thwart the ghostly chef's interference. Not every problem is solved so easily. The chef continues to haunt the kitchen of the Furnace Creek Inn.

Whaley House

Like the Winchester House, the Whaley House bears the distinction of having been certified as haunted by the US government. It seems that in the 1960s to 1970s the US Department of Commerce was looking for ways to increase tourism when someone hit upon the idea of ghosts. Thus, a brochure was created listing locations that were supposedly haunted. In 2005 *Life* magazine went so far as to call the Whaley House the most haunted house in America. And that's quite a reputation to live up to. But not to worry, the Whaley House really is haunted.

Completed in 1857 the Whaley House was one of San Diego's first two-story brick houses. A house that Thomas Whaley was so proud of he claimed it to be the finest home within 150 miles. Over time the house would serve also as a theater and the San Diego County Courthouse in 1869, for which Whaley was paid sixty-five dollars per month. But it was the 1852 execution by hanging of Yankee Jim (Santiago) Robinson on the property that led to the most ghostly activity.

Robinson stole a boat for which he was convicted of grand larceny and sentenced to death. His hanging was horrible. The noose was placed around his neck as he sat in a wagon. Yankee Jim tried desperately to stay in the wagon but it was pushed from him, and according to witnesses his neck wasn't broken. Instead, he swung like a pendulum until he slowly strangled to death. Witnessing the hanging was Thomas Whaley; however, the spectacle didn't deter him from purchasing the same plot of land and building his house upon it. If only he'd known that the ghostly Yankee Jim came along with the land.

Soon after the Whaleys moved in, there were the sounds of heavy footsteps that could be heard throughout the house. Thomas Whaley was convinced that Yankee Jim still haunted the location of his execution. Whaley probably never thought that one day he and his wife, Anna, and their daughter, Violet, would join Yankee Jim in residence at the Whaley House. The ghostly Whaleys have been seen numerous times since the Whaley House was opened as a museum in 1960. The aroma of cigar smoke signals the presence of Mr. Whaley, usually spotted at the top of the staircase. Mrs. Whaley has been seen in the garden and on the first floor.

The unfortunate Violet was as much a victim of the time in which she lived as she was of the scheming George T. Bertolacci who married her for her money. After a few weeks of marriage, he ran off and left his twenty-two-year-old bride. Heartbroken and filled with humiliation, Violet found herself an outcast of polite Victorian society when she returned to live with her parents at the family home. The Bertolaccis divorced a year later and Violet sunk into a deeper depression. On August 18, 1885, she sat down and scribbled a hasty suicide note:

Mad from life's history
Swift to death's mystery
Glad to be hurled
Anywhere, anywhere, out of this world

And then she picked up her father's 32-caliber rifle and shot herself in the heart. Little did she know that the *anywhere out of the world* would see her as a permanent and very ghostly resident in the garden of the Whaley House. She may have a ghostly canine companion. The Whaleys had a little dog they called Dolly Varden. Dolly is drawn to children, who usually see her running about the house.

In 1964 TV personality Regis Philbin and a friend spent the night at the Whaley House at the suggestion of noted ghost hunter Hans Holzer. A dark and stormy night, they set out to dispel the idea of ghosts. After witnessing what they believed was a ghost, they came away with a very different mind-set.

My ghost hunting friend Eric Sellers has investigated hauntings around the world. During a recent conversation on California ghosts, he told me the following experiences while visiting the Whaley House in 2007 and 2008:

If you ask me I'd say the Whaley House is one of California's very active locations. In 2007 I was at the Whaley House for a seminar and I was standing on the porch with a lady when I looked into the window. I was looking through sheers (curtains) but I could still see very well. There was no one in the room, but all of sudden the rocking chair started to rock. Back and forth like someone was sitting in it. Later I was inside and tried to debunk what I'd seen. I tried everything to get that chair to rock, jumping up and down on the floor and breathing hard at it. Nothing happened. That chair would not rock.

This happened in 2008: You know that long hallway upstairs? I was up there and walked past the theater and then on down the hall. As I passed the nursery, I heard little kids, like toddlers giggling and laughing. I stopped and stepped back, thinking some kids had got in there, even though there was a railing. But there was nobody in that room.

El Campo Santo Cemetery

*A*bout two blocks from the Whaley House is El Campo Santo (the Holy Fields) Cemetery, San Diego's second oldest cemetery. Where most cemeteries are closed behind locked gates after dark, El Campo Santo is accessible anytime, day or night. With the passage of time, the city has grown up around the cemetery so that restaurants, bars, and residences are the old cemetery's neighbors. And the tales they tell are of electrical disturbances, disembodied voices, mournful cries, car alarms going off for no reason, cars that won't start, and the fleeting shadowy figures of both men and women. Apparently, everyone doesn't rest at peace here.

The cemetery opened on November 8, 1849, with the burial of Juan Adams. For the next thirty-one years Adams would be followed by 477 other residents of old town San Diego. Yankee Jim is one of them. Although he lies here at El Campo Santo, Yankee Jim much prefers haunting the location where he was hanged, the Whaley House.

Legend has it that the old gravedigger of Campo Santo, Rafael Mamudes (one hundred years old), murdered his wife and spent the rest of his long life doing penance for his terrible deed. As an act of contrition he rang the church bells and dug the graves. According to a 1909 article in the *San Francisco Call* newspaper, the reclusive Rafael lived in a house near the cemetery. The article referred to his house as the house of one hundred coffins. All of San Diego called old Rafael's little house the coffin house. Its front door was a coffin box lid and it was decorated with broken coffins and bits and pieces of other funerary items. And yet, the old man was never accused of grave robbing. However, he was said to share his house with ghosts. Perhaps he found them more companionable. After he died old Rafael Mamudes joined his ghostly pals in refusing to vacate the premises.

He is most often seen roaming El Campo Santo late at night. You will know him when you see the stooped, little old man with wild, flowing hair. Speak to him if you will, but be warned: In life he rarely spoke to, or acknowledged, anyone, and as a ghost Rafael will ignore you.

The moaning ghost who appears to be in the most distress may be Thomas Wrightington. His headstone tells it all. Wrightington "fell from his horse and was nearly eaten up by coyotes."

The small cemetery we see today is not nearly as large as it once was. We can blame this on progress and the toll it took. Public transportation has always been important. Even in 1889 when a streetcar line was built through the cemetery. There is also the fact that the boundary of El Campo Santo was moved and paved over in the early 1940s. This left some of the cemetery's residents outside the cemetery—and under San Diego Avenue, Linwood Street, and the sidewalk.

As you walk along this area, you will see the small metal markers (dots) that read "grave site." The grave sites were discovered in 1993 when ground penetrating radar was brought to El Campo Santo and used to locate graves outside the cemetery.

A plaque on the wall of El Camp Santo explains:

> Remembering the more than 20 Men, Women and Children who lie buried beneath San Diego Ave. Only Assemblyman Edward L. Greene was exhumed and placed within the new boundary of El Campo Santo Cemetery. These graves were discovered with the use of ground penetrating radar in 1993. Rest In Peace. This plaque was placed by the Historical Shrine Foundation with funds from the San Diego Community Block Grant in 1994.

The White Deer of Presidio Park

The original Mission San Diego de Alcalá was established on July 16, 1769, by Father Junipero Serra at Presidio Hill in what is Presidio Park today. It was the first of the twenty-one Franciscan missions that were founded in California. The nearby presidio was California's first fort. Don't look for ruins here. Today there is nothing left of the old fort and the mission at Presidio Park.

According to local lore, the ghost in Presidio Park is that of Lucy, the white deer. Lucy and her brother were born at the Los Angeles County Zoo in 1965. Rare in the fact that they were both white, Lucy and her brother were sold to a family that lived near Presidio Park in the early 1970s. Shortly afterward the brother disappeared and was never seen again. But Lucy continued to thrive, foraging on vegetation at Presidio Park or neighbors' flower beds.

Lucy died in 1975 when it was decided that the deer should be moved to a safer area and an animal control officer over-estimated the amount of tranquilizer needed to sedate her. Anger was swift. A monument was placed in honor of Lucy with the following words: Bliss in solitude beneath this tree, Formless, silent, spirit free.

But Lucy liked this area and decided to stay on. The ghostly white deer's favorite time to roam is at dusk. She often startles those who don't know her story, as she scampers into the bushes in Presidio Park as they approach.

Death at Mission San Diego de Alcalá

In 1774 the Mission San Diego de Alcalá was relocated to what is known as Mission Valley in order to separate the church from the presidio. Today the church is an active parish church. Many who've visited the church claim it is haunted by the ghost of Father Luis Jayme, a long-ago priest who lost his life here.

During the early morning hours of November 4, 1775, the good padre was awakened by the smell of smoke. He rushed outside to see what was happening, not realizing that a murderous mob was waiting.

"Amar a Dios, mis hijos (Love God, my children)," he called out to them. Those were the last words he ever spoke. The band of angry men rushed him, pulling his clothing off, stabbing him, and battering him until he fell dead there on the mission grounds. He is entombed beneath the floor of the sanctuary. Is he the ghostly gray padre who's been spotted over the years in and around the church? Some believe the ghost who walks the grounds with a lighted candle in one hand and a cross in the other is indeed Father Luis Jayme. If anyone stares at him too long, he will vanish right before their startled eyes. Otherwise the ghostly padre goes about his business seemingly unaware that several centuries have come and gone since he came here to California from his beloved Majorca.

Villa Montezuma

The Villa Montezuma in San Diego is rumored to be both haunted and cursed. Today it is known as the Villa Montezuma Museum. There is no denying that it certainly looks the part of a haunted house, although the museum says it is not haunted but enchanted. And judging by its history, that could well be.

The original owner of Villa Montezuma was renowned Spiritualist composer/pianist Jesse Shepard, who came to San Diego by way of Europe. It was in Europe where Shepard enjoyed fame as a brilliant pianist and performed before many celebrities of the era and heads of state that included author Alexander Dumas, the czar of Russia, and the prince of Wales. It was believed that Shepard's ability at composing and playing was channeled from the great composers. It was widely rumored that Shepard could channel two different composers while playing the piano.

While visiting the czar of Russia, Shepard learned how to conduct séances. It was a knowledge that would bring him even more recognition. Two Spiritualist brothers offered Jesse Shepard a house, built to his specifications, if he would relocate to San Diego. For all his fame, Shepard was never wealthy; he readily agreed. And in 1887 the Villa Montezuma was built to suit him, complete with music room and séance room. It is said that Shepard, who could mimic the sounds of different instruments with his voice, gave concerts for the spirits in the music room and the séance room.

Tiring of Spiritualism and music, Shepard turned his attention to writing and took up the pen name Francis Grierson. A year later he took out a mortgage for the Villa Montezuma and used the proceeds to finance a move to Paris with his companion, Lawrence Tonner. There his first book was published. Shepard's greatest literary success would come several years later with *The Valley of Shadows*.

Jesse Shepard and Lawrence Tonner returned to San Diego a few years later and sold the Villa Montezuma. But their financial situation was such that they lived in poverty throughout the rest of their lives.

On Sunday, May 29, 1927, Jesse Shepard and Lawrence Tonner were invited to dinner at a friend's home. After dinner Shepard agreed to entertain his host with a piano recital. He sat down and began to play. As his hands struck the last chord, the music ended and he stopped. But something was wrong. And Lawrence Tonner realized it. He jumped up and ran to Shepard, who had died after striking the last chord.

Several years ago my husband, Bill, and I took a tour of San Diego's haunted spots. One of the tour's stops was the Villa Montezuma. It was not quite dusk when we entered the parlor. Before the tour guide said a word about the Villa Montezuma's history, we shivered in the room's chill, although it was summer. Glancing around the room at the magnificent stained-glass windows, I felt a sense of oppression and sadness. And here I'll add that I am no more sensitive than the next person. Yet, the experience was so overwhelming that even our brief visit to the Villa Montezuma all those years ago left a lasting impression on me.

Later when Bill and I discussed the tour, he agreed that the Villa Montezuma was the most impressive site we'd stopped at. But it is more than that. There is a belief among paranormal researchers that those who are intensely gifted mediums exist on a different stratum from the rest of us, and that they can leave an indelible imprint on places they knew and loved in life. Jesse Shepard/Francis Grierson was just such a person. And when you step into his home, the Villa Montezuma, you will know that haunted, cursed, or enchanted, Jesse Shepard is there.

The Pink Lady of Yorba Linda Cemetery

The Yorba Linda Cemetery sits amidst a modern neighborhood in Yorba Linda. Established by Don Bernardo Yorba in 1858, it is the oldest private cemetery in Orange County. And yes, there is a ghost associated with the Yorba Linda Cemetery. She is known as the Pink Lady and has been talked about for decades. Her identity is a mystery.

Legend has it that the Pink Lady is the ghost of Alvina de los Reyes, a descendant of Don Bernardo Yorba. Alvina, who died in a carriage accident on her way home from a dance, was wearing a pink gown at the time of her death, and as a specter she has chosen to appear in pink. The ghostly Pink Lady is said to appear only in the hours after midnight on June 15 and only on even numbered years. This, some say, marks the anniversary of her death. Every year crowds gather at the grave of Alvina de los Reyes at the Yorba Linda Cemetery to await her appearance.

There are those who insist they've witnessed the Pink Lady ghost slowly walking among the headstones in the historic old cemetery. Then there are the skeptics who insist that while Alvina de los Reyes was a real person who died in childbirth, she was not a young girl who died on her way home from a dance. The story, they say, is nothing but an unverifiable old legend. The only way to know for sure is to visit the Yorba Linda Cemetery on June 15 and see for yourself if the Pink Lady ghost chooses to take a lonely walk among the headstones.

Walt's on the Premises

*W*alt Disney gave the world Mickey Mouse—and a slew of unforgettable characters such as Donald Duck, Goofy, and Pluto. Disney was a visionary. A writer, an animator, and film producer, Walt Disney pointed animation in a new direction in 1937 with the first full-length cel animated film *Snow White and the Seven Dwarfs*. A critical and a commercial success, the film was only the beginning for Walt Disney. In 1955 he gave the world Disneyland, "The Happiest Place on Earth." Over seven hundred million people have visited Disneyland since its official opening on July 17, 1955. Some of them have never left, and may well be haunting the park to this day. They are in good company—the ghostly Walt Disney has been seen in and around the park since his death in 1966.

As Disneyland was being built, Walt Disney had an apartment built above the fire station on Main Street, USA. Designed to his specifications, the apartment was kept as a place for him and his family to relax within the park. Whenever Disney was at the park, he kept a lamp turned on in the window to signal his presence. The day after his death the lamp was turned off. However, the lamp was turned on again within the week—and remains lit.

The apartment may still be Walt Disney's favorite place at Disneyland. According to those who've seen him, the ghostly Disney stands at the window near the lamp and happily watches visitors as they walk along Main Street, USA. There have also been sightings of Disney at the Sleeping Beauty Castle and at the Pirates of the Caribbean entrance. Those who've encountered him say he is happy and smiling. Others believe Disney is the ghostly man who walks a lonely path after the park is closed for the day.

The ghostly Lady in White died at this location a century before Walt Disney dreamt of Disneyland. A kindly ghost, she helps lost children find their way to their parents on Main Street, USA. But like any other place on earth, Disneyland is not immune to accidents. Is it the stuff of urban legend or fact? Some people claim to have encountered the ghosts of guests who died in tragic accidents while enjoying the park. They are said to haunt the rides and the areas where they met their terrible ends. That's something to think about next time you climb into the Matterhorn Bobsleds or a doom buggy at the Haunted Mansion.

Strange as it may seem, there are those who visit Disneyland with the sole purpose of depositing the cremains of loved ones. The preferred location for this is the Haunted Mansion. That just seems so outré. Wouldn't the Sleeping Beauty Castle be more appropriate?

Sadly, suicide and murder have also come to Disneyland. On different occasions four men leapt to their deaths from a top-floor balcony of the Disneyland Hotel. In March 1981 eighteen-year-old Mel Yorba was stabbed to death by James O'Driscoll in Tomorrowland. Driscoll claimed Yorba had acted inappropriately with his girlfriend. Six years later a gang fight broke out in the parking lot. When the shooting stopped and the smoke cleared, a fifteen-year-old gang member was discovered to have been shot to death. Clearly, Walt Disney is probably not alone in haunting Disneyland.

Amargosa Hotel and Opera House

*L*ocated in Death Valley, the Amargosa Hotel and Opera House was a broken-down old building when ballerina, artist, and actress Marta Becket happened across it in 1967. Clearly both the Amargosa and Becket benefited from that chance meeting. Becket was traveling across the country with her husband, and doing her one-woman show in small town theaters. She liked what she saw at the Amargosa. Here is where she belonged. And here is where she settled. She slowly transformed the place.

Over the years Marta Becket was sought out by writers and photographers for her perspective about this unique place in the desert. How, they wondered, could a ballerina from New York be happy here in the isolation of Death Valley? Some say that Marta Becket brought ghosts to the opera house when she painted an audience on the walls. Others say it's always been haunted.

My ghost-hunting friend Debbie Hollingsworth and I attended a ghost conference at the Amargosa a number of years ago while Marta Becket was still alive. It was early March and already things in Death Valley were heating up. We drove through the day to finally reach the hotel. As we checked in, we saw that clearly, the hotel's best days were long gone; sadness pervaded the place. We'd been told that this was a hot spot for Hollywood sorts back in the day. But looking around we couldn't help but wonder just how comfortable our room would be.

We greeted other attendees and saw just how giddy they were at the prospect of investigating the Spooky Hollow area of the hotel later that night. They knew something about this place that we didn't. Some of them were regulars. And this was the first time here for both of us. We were scheduled to conduct a séance in Spooky Hollow before the investigation, but after a walk through we agreed that this would not be a good place for a séance. There were some in the group who disagreed with the decision, but the negative pall that hung over Spooky Hollow like a blanket was just too strong to ignore. Whatever spirits were here would not be kind or cooperative. We were told that a janitor had committed suicide in this area and grew angry and agitated with ghost investigators. And so we scrubbed the séance and focused on the opera house.

The audiences that Marta Becket painted on the walls and the lighting lend eeriness to the opera house. Nonetheless we were successful in gathering EVP, and Debbie did quite well communicating with ghosts through automatic writing. It's been said that by painting audiences on the wall, Marta Becket caused ghosts to be trapped here. We had no sense of this; we agreed that the ghosts here seemed friendlier and more accepting than those at Spooky Hollow.

Sometime later Zak Bagans and his *Ghost Adventures* TV show came to investigate the Amargosa. No doubt they encountered a lot of angry ghosts. And they are welcome to them.

About the comfort of our room—little did we know we'd been given one of the most haunted rooms at the hotel. The room was a lot of things, but comfortable wasn't one of them, especially with the rappings, knockings, and disembodied voices that emanated there. Here let me say that unlike most ghost investigators, I don't like sleeping in a haunted room. Invariably I have disturbing dreams. And this night was no exception. I woke at one point to see a spirit come through one side of the room and exit out the other. It was late, and I was tired of ghosts. So I pretended not to notice him and went back to sleep.

Tricky Dick

*U*nlike Abe Lincoln, not all presidential ghosts take up residence at the White House. Richard "Tricky Dick" Nixon is one who chooses to haunt his birthplace, his grave, and the presidential library at Yorba Linda rather than the Oval Office at 1600 Pennsylvania Avenue. Remembering that Nixon left the White House in disgrace, this is understandable. If not for his successor, Gerald Ford, issuing a full pardon—but that's a different story.

Richard Milhous Nixon was born in Southern California in 1913. After several years in politics, most notably as vice president to Dwight D. Eisenhower, and an unsuccessful 1960 run as president in which he lost to John F. Kennedy, Nixon finally won a presidential election in 1968. He won a second term by a large landslide in 1972, and this is where he got into trouble and earned the nickname Tricky Dick. The scandal was called Watergate, and Nixon resigned in disgrace from the office of president on August 9, 1974. He died twenty years later on April 22, 1994.

Nixon is buried beside his wife, Pat, at the presidential library and his birthplace in Yorba Linda. And if the rumors are true, both Nixons are very much in residence here. They've appeared near their graves and walking together in the rose garden. Some who've witnessed the ghostly president and first lady say they look much as they did in life. Others say they appear only as glowing green mists.

This seems reasonable considering the Nixon family put on the first Halloween party ever at the White House. Granted this was a kiddies' event and nothing like the Halloween parties of today with ghosts and vampires in starring roles. Still, Halloween was reportedly the Nixon family's favorite holiday. And that is impressive.

Blood Alley: James Dean on Highway 46

*S*eptember 30, 1955, fell on a Friday. The last day of the work week and the last day of the month. Thirteen days earlier, twenty-four-year-old actor and pop idol James Dean had filmed a PSA about speeding for the National Highway Safety Committee. At the end of the thirty-second commercial, Dean looked at the camera and said, "Take it easy driving. The life you save might be mine."

On this Friday, James Dean and his friend and mechanic Rolf Wütherich met up with friends who would follow along in other vehicles at the Ranch Market on Vine Street. The group enjoyed donuts and coffee before heading north toward Salinas and a sports car race competition. It was 1:15 in the afternoon. Salinas was about 260 miles away; if Dean pushed the Porsche Spyder they would arrive before the others did.

Two hours into the trip near Bakersfield, Dean was stopped by a highway patrol officer and given a speeding ticket. Afterward he turned the Porsche onto State Route 46 (old Highway 466) and continued speeding as he drove west. Near Cholame, college student Donald Turnupseed pulled his Ford Tudor onto the highway heading east. It was 5:45 in the afternoon. At what is now called the Cholame Y intersection, Turnupseed slowed the Ford and tried to make a left turn. There was no way James Dean could avoid the fatal head-on collision. He died en route to the hospital. Rolf Wütherich was thrown from the car and although severely injured, he would survive. This location is now known as the James Dean Memorial Junction. Opposite the memorial junction sign is the Jack Ranch Café with its steel and glass James Dean memorial.

James Dean is the most famous person to die here but he is not the only one. People have perished in horrific head-on collisions and accidents ever since Dean's death. And because of all those fatalities on this stretch of Highway 46, it is referred to as Blood Alley. Much like Abe Lincoln's ghost train, a ghostly Porsche Spyder is said to cruise down this area in the early predawn hours. Behind the wheel is the ghost of James Dean. Imagine the shock of a motorist cruising down the highway when the Porsche Spyder suddenly appears up ahead. It's happened, according to some.

Others have reportedly seen the glowing apparition of James Dean walking along the highway near his memorial. He is a forlorn figure, appearing much as he did when he played Jim Stark in *Rebel Without a Cause*. As is the case with many who die suddenly and unexpectedly, the ghostly James Dean may wonder just what went wrong.

Dona Petronilla and Her Curse

Los Angeles's Griffith Park is the city's showpiece. Located within the park are the Griffith Observatory, the Los Angeles Zoo, the Autry Museum of the American West, and the Greek Theater. The park is also a place for enjoying nature with its many walking trails and horse-riding trails. At 4,310 acres Griffith Park is far larger than either New York's Central Park or San Francisco's Golden Gate Park. Murder has occurred at all three parks, and all are haunted. However, Griffith Park, unlike the other two urban parks, is also cursed.

It all began in 1863 with the death of Don Antonio Feliz. Feliz was a wealthy landowner whose family was granted the land that is currently Griffith Park. Living with Señor Feliz were his sister and her daughter, Petronilla. Pampered Petronilla wanted for nothing. Hers was a fine and comfortable life. That all changed when Señor Feliz died of smallpox and left all his land not to his sister, nor to Petronilla. Don Coronel and his lawyer Don Innocante visited Señor Feliz on his deathbed, and tricked him into leaving his land to Coronel.

Suddenly homeless, Petronilla and her mother were devastated. Seventeen-year-old Petronilla was furious at Don Coronel. She tried to regain her rightful property. But the judge threw out the case, finding that the will was legal and binding. Powerless to change her fate, she placed a curse on Coronel, Innocante, and the land. In his 1930 posthumously published book, *On the Old West Coast,* Major Horace Bell repeated Petronilla's curse:

> Your falsity shall be your ruin! The substance of the Feliz family shall be your curse! The lawyer that assisted you in your infamy, and the judge, shall fall beneath the same curse. The one shall die an untimely death and the other in blood and violence. A blight shall fall on this terrestrial paradise. The cattle shall

sicken, the fields shall no longer respond to the til-
ler. I see a great flood spreading destruction. I see the
grand oaks wither in the tongues of flames. The wrath
of heaven and the vengeance of hell shall fall upon
this place.

Some stories say Petronilla dropped dead immediately after issuing the curse. Others have her living to a ripe old age. Either way,
the curse fell upon those who'd cheated Petronilla, until the land
fell into the hands of Griffith J. Griffith. Griffith gave the land to the
City of Los Angeles, some say, as a way to avoid the curse's aim. And
here again Horace Bell tells of the dinner the city staged in honor of
Griffith and his gift.

According to Bell, the ghost of Don Antonio Feliz appeared at the
dinner inviting the guests to dine with him in hell. "In your great
honor I have brought an escort of sub-demons," the ghostly Feliz
said. Needless to say, the dinner party was a miserable failure, as
one by one the guests ran from the dining room and out the door.

But we must remember that Horace Bell, like Mark Twain,
tended to embellish his stories. Perhaps the ghostly Don Antonio
Feliz never made an appearance at a dinner party. Perhaps Dona
Petronilla never issued a curse either. And yet, there is that ghostly
woman clad in a luminous white gown, her long, dark hair billowing
out behind her as she rides her white stallion through Griffith Park
on moonlit nights. Is she Dona Petronilla?

Greystone and its Ghosts

*G*reat wealth is no guarantee against tragedy. So it was with the Edward L. Doheny family. Doheny and his partner Charles A. Canfield changed Los Angeles forever in 1892 with their discovery of oil (near the present-day La Brea Tar Pits).

Suddenly Edward L. Doheny was one of the wealthiest men in the US. He and his wife, Carrie, moved into a new and grander home. It was nothing when compared to the home their only son, Edward L. Doheny Jr. (Ned), would have built on the twelve-and-a-half-acre parcel of land they gave him as a wedding gift in 1926.

The magnificent forty-six-thousand-square-foot Greystone Mansion was completed at a cost of nearly three million dollars, the most expensive home in California at that time. On the grounds were a swimming pool, tennis courts, kennels, stables, and all the trappings the very wealthy might expect and enjoy. In September 1928 Ned; his wife, Lucy; and their five children happily moved in. Five months later tragedy struck.

February 16, 1929, Ned Doheny was discovered in a guest bedroom shot to death. Nearby was the body of his longtime personal friend and assistant Hugh Plunkett. What happened? Rumors were rampant. Were Ned and Hugh lovers? Had Lucy walked in on them and enraged, she shot them both? Were their deaths the result of a lovers' quarrel, one shooting the other? Or had Hugh Plunkett simply shot his friend and employer then turned the gun on himself? The murder weapon belonged to Ned Doheny. And yet, the circumstances surrounding the two deaths are as much a mystery today as they were on the night they occurred.

Over the years several people have seen the ghost of Lucy as she fitfully makes her way from room to room. There is also the ghostly man who aimlessly wanders the halls of Greystone Mansion. No one is sure if he is the ghost of Ned Doheny or Hugh Plunkett. The identity of the ghostly man in black is also a mystery. But he's been spotted roaming Greystone Mansion numerous times. Perhaps these restless ghosts roam the mansion in hopes of setting the record straight and righting a terrible wrong.

Ma Duncan at Ventura City Hall

Built in 1912–1913, the Ventura City Hall originally served as the Ventura County Courthouse, sheriff's office, and jail. The building was closed in 1969 and sold to the City of Ventura. After much restoration, retro-fitting, and structural reinforcement, it began a new life as the Ventura City Hall in 1974. Apparently, the ghosts here decided to stay on.

Never doubt that this old building at 501 Poli Street is haunted. Repurposed or not, imagine being in the old courthouse after everyone else has gone home for the day. The sights and sounds that happen here are sometimes unnerving. We know the murderess Ma Duncan is long dead. Apparently, she doesn't know this. Coming face to face with a spectral killer is not an easy thing. But the matronly looking Elizabeth Ann Duncan, aka Ma, has been seen in and around the old courthouse ever since her death.

Duncan was one of the defendants in the most famous trial to have taken place within the courthouse. Charged with the horrific murder of her daughter-in-law, Olga Kupczyk, Duncan took the stand in her own defense and denied any part in the slaying. But there were too many people who knew Duncan too well—and they testified against her. After deliberating fifty-one minutes, the jury found Duncan guilty and she was sentenced to death.

Her attorney son fought to save her—to no avail. On August 8, 1962, Elizabeth Duncan became the fourth and final woman to ever be executed by the State of California when she took her seat in the gas chamber at San Quentin.

Duncan, aka Ma, was the mother-in-law from hell. A grasping woman who just couldn't stand to let her only son go. At fifty-four Ma Duncan was recovering from a suicide attempt and needed a nurse when into her life walked pretty young nurse Olga Kupczyk. It might have been okay if only Ma's son, Frank, hadn't fallen for Olga.

Olga was likewise impressed with Frank and a romance ensued. Knowing his mother's insane jealousy, Frank and Olga sneaked off and secretly wed on June 20, 1958. When Ma found out she was furious. But she had a plan. She paid a young man to impersonate her son, and posing as her daughter-in-law, Ma and the man appeared at the Ventura courthouse and had *their* marriage annulled.

Things went from bad to worse when six months into the marriage, Olga announced her pregnancy. Ma had another plan. She hired thugs to kidnap and kill Olga, thus ending her hold and that of her unborn child on Frank. And that's what they did. The two men kidnapped Olga, took her to a deserted area, beat her, and left her for dead in a shallow grave.

Perhaps Duncan's ghost is held here in penitence for the callous murder of her daughter-in-law. Maybe she seeks a retrial with the ghostly judge who also happens to be in residence. Whatever her reasons, the ghostly Duncan walks these halls.

She is not alone; there are unexplained cold drafts that are reported in some areas of the building, and the elevator seems to have a mind of its own, transporting spectral passengers from one floor to the next. Its usual destination is the third floor where a chicly dressed woman waits impatiently. What's her hurry? Doesn't time cease to exist in the spirit world?

Hollywood Roosevelt Hotel

*T*he Hollywood Roosevelt Hotel is said to be the most haunted hotel in Los Angeles. And it probably is. The twelve-story Hollywood Roosevelt Hotel opened on May 15, 1927, two years before the Great Depression and before California implemented income tax for its residents. True, it was the height of Prohibition, but that didn't stop the Hollywood set from enjoying the grand new hotel and flowing bootleg liquor. Celebrity has its perks. No wonder so many ghostly stars are associated with the Hollywood Roosevelt Hotel.

In the early 1950s before the blonde newcomer took the name Marilyn Monroe, she posed for a magazine ad at the hotel's pool. Star quality, charisma, whatever magic that pushes one into the limelight—she had it. She lightened her hair a few shades, changed her name, and the rest is showbiz history. The Roosevelt was Marilyn's favorite hotel. Her suite of choice was Suite 1200, poolside. With her fame skyrocketing, Marilyn stayed here for two years. Her only demand was that a full-length mirror be placed in the suite during her stay. Years after her death, the spectral Marilyn is still making an appearance in that mirror, which was moved to various locations within the hotel. It is usually in Suite 1200 or near an elevator. According to those who've seen her, Marilyn's ghost sometimes occupies Suite 1200.

Carole Lombard is another celebrity who has taken up residence at the Hollywood Roosevelt. On her way home to her husband, Clark Gable, Lombard died in a fiery plane crash on January 16, 1942, at Mt. Potosi near Las Vegas. It's said that ghosts will often return to those places where they enjoyed their greatest happiness. For Lombard one of those places was the twelfth floor of the Hollywood Roosevelt. She and Clark Gable were in love and happy there. Although she is often seen here, Gable is not. Make of that what you will.

Montgomery Clift haunts Room 928—he and his trumpet. During filming of *From Here to Eternity*, Clift stayed here at the Hollywood Roosevelt. And much to the displeasure of other guests, Clift practiced his trumpet, playing late into the night.

You'd think that after all these years Clift would have improved his ability with the trumpet. According to those who've heard him, he hasn't. This begs the question, is Montgomery Clift and his trumpet an intelligent haunting that can interact and respond, or is he merely a residual haunting, imprinted on the surroundings much like the loop sequence of a film, with no awareness playing over and over?

Down in the ballroom a distinctive chill fills the room as ghostly partygoers in ermine, jewels, and tuxes appear on occasion. The aroma of smoke and gardenias wafts through the air, and faint sounds of Big Band era music echo through the emptiness, accompanied by the tinkle of glasses and laughter. Perhaps being a celebrity means never having to leave the party.

Naked Natalie

Natalie Wood was one of four young actors who starred in *Rebel Without a Cause*. All four met untimely ends, and except for Natalie, they died before reaching the zenith of their careers. Natalie Wood lived to be forty-three; the others died in their twenties and thirties. Some might say Wood was the lucky one. But was she?

It was well known that Natalie Wood was terrified of water. And yet in the middle of the bay on a dark and cold November night, dressed only in a gown and a parka, she is said to have boarded a dingy leaving her and husband Robert Wagner's yacht, the *Splendour*, behind. Her body was discovered a mile from the yacht, several hours later. She had drowned. Her death was ruled an accident. And that may well be. But then again, what if it wasn't? If not, who was responsible for Natalie Wood's death? Those are questions we're not likely ever to see answered. Forty years later, the actress's death remains a mystery. And that brings us to the ghost.

The beautiful star died in the waters off Catalina Island. An unexpected, violent, and mysterious death often gives rise to a haunting. Natalie Wood's death checked all those boxes. It wasn't long after her death that the ghostly Natalie Wood made an appearance. Interestingly, she appears differently to different people. Some have seen her dressed in a gauzy white gown, walking along the beach at Catalina as if in a trance. Others have witnessed Natalie, sans clothing, strolling down the beach. This naked Natalie, they say, seems to be the most content ghost on Catalina. Perhaps she has found happiness in the afterlife and has come to terms with the way her untimely death occurred.

The Bride, the Stage, and the White Horse of Vallecito Station

Situated in California's Colorado Desert, the Vallecito Station was a stop on the old Butterfield Stage route. The area here in the low desert is fraught with legends of murder, ghosts, and treasure somewhere in the rocky canyons, just waiting to be discovered. It's said that a bandit running from a posse stopped in this area to rest with his wife. When he realized that he wasn't going to survive, the bandit went out among the boulders and hid his stolen bag of gold coins. He died a short time later, leaving his wife to search for the coins. She never found them.

Sometime in the mid-1800s the legend of the ghost bride of Vallecito Station began. As the story goes, a young woman was traveling by stagecoach from her home on the East Coast to Northern California where she planned to marry her lover. Along the way, she became violently ill and died near Vallecito. Because no one knew her name, she was buried in an unmarked grave. The beautiful white wedding dress that she'd so carefully packed and carried with her was used as her burial dress.

The young woman's story was just another desert tragedy—until she began appearing at Vallecito Station. The spectral bride always appears in her white wedding gown. When the night is calm and stars twinkle across a moonless sky, a ghostly black stallion comes galloping toward the old station. Those who have seen her astride the stallion say that the air takes a bone-chilling drop as she nears Vallecito Station. Neither she nor the stallion makes a sound. Other times, the ghostly bride leaves her horse behind and appears at the Vallecito Station pacing back and forth.

Out on Carrizo Wash the ghostly coach races toward safety and oblivion. The story goes that the lone driver was attacked and killed by robbers, intent on taking the box of gold coins that was aboard the coach. The thieves hid the gold, intending to return for it later. Try as they might they were never able to locate their ill-gotten loot. The spectral white stallion that's seen galloping through the region on full moon nights belonged to one of the thieves. The men became so enraged at not being able to find the coins that they shot and killed one another. The white stallion ran off into the hills only to return as a ghost.

The ghostly stagecoach continues making an occasional appearance as a reminder of the event. Its driver is a skeleton, cracking the whip as his spectral team of horses pulls the phantom coach across the desert sand. The skeleton driver of the coach is not to be confused with the eight-foot skeleton that appears with a lantern in its chest. The unusually tall skeleton is believed to be that of an old miner who found and forgot a gold mine in this area. He takes on this menacing form to frighten anyone who happens to get too close to his claim.

It's quiet and peaceful out here in the desert. Today the Vallecito Station sits within the Vallecito County Park in the Anza Borrego State Park. There are forty-four primitive campsites, restrooms, and showers—and yes, the ghosts.

Char Man and the Heedless, Headless Hog Rider of Camp Comfort

*R*ock and roll was music to teenage ears, color television was a rarity, and Marlon Brando as Johnny Strabler was an outlaw biker in the film *The Wild One*—this was the early 1950s. Brando was considered cool in his t-shirt, jeans, and leather jacket. A man many wanted to emulate. It may have been around this time that Char Man of Ojai's Creek Road made his first appearance.

Described as a grotesquely bandaged, foul-smelling man-creature, Char Man comes out of the woods late at night with evil on his mind. He is no friendly ghost. Char Man has been known to try to get into cars that are stopped. He will also taunt and chase those who come looking for him. If he should grab anyone, Char Man pulls them into the woods—never to be seen again.

In spite of his reputation, ghost investigators regularly come out to Creek Road Bridge hoping to catch a glimpse of the hideously disfigured Char Man. Not as elusive is the spectral Harley rider who races down Ojai's Creek Road near Camp Comfort.

Sometime in the early 1950s a man took his new Harley out for a late-night ride. A warm fall night, a full moon overhead, and an endless empty road ahead of him, he happily sped down Creek Road. He may have even imagined himself to be like Brando, all swagger and self-assurance, ignoring speed limits and warning signs. His was not the only vehicle on the road that night. Up ahead a large truck was cruising along obeying the speed limit. No matter, the truck was moving much too slowly for the Harley rider.

He had no intention of crawling along the road at twenty-five miles an hour. There was no one else on the road. He pulled out to pass the truck. This was not going to be his night. Just as the Harley came up even with the truck's cab, something broke from the truck, decapitating and killing the Harley rider instantly.

He still takes his Harley out for a late-night ride. And unlike Char Man, the ghostly Harley rider won't attack you. He is here in search of his head. If you should be out on Creek Road late some night and see a single headlight in the distance, slow down and let him pass.

Hollywood

A Ghost Walks at the Chinese Theater

If some locations are more haunted than others, theaters would be at the top of the list. None would be more so than the historic TCL Chinese Theater. The ever-popular tourist attraction started life as Grauman's Chinese Theater in 1927 with the premier of Cecil B. DeMille's epic silent film *The King of Kings*. Designated as a Los Angeles Historic Cultural Monument in 1968, the TCL Chinese Theater is not only famous for being a movie theater, but for the concrete handprints and footprints of Hollywood notables out front of the building.

The first theater to offer air conditioning, Grauman's quickly became an elegant place for film producers to showcase their latest film. Howard Hughes held the world premiere of his 1929 war film *Hells Angels* at Grauman's in 1930. The 1944, 1945, and 1946 Academy Awards ceremonies were held at Grauman's as well. With all this film history, and all the celebrities and Hollywood moguls spending time here, you might think that one or two of them would have stuck around the theater. Apparently, this isn't the case.

The ghost in the TCL Chinese Theater is that of a little girl. Why she has chosen to haunt the Chinese Theater is anybody's guess. Mine would be that the child lived and died in this area long before there was a theater, and she is comfortable here. Think of everything she's seen and heard here. She loves to play in the curtains and startles those who encounter her only because no one is expecting to run into a ghostly little girl in the empty theater.

The other ghost associated with the TCL Chinese Theater is that of elderly character actor Victor Kilian, whose brutal March 11, 1979, murder has never been solved. Kilian lived near the theater and often walked to nearby bars to socialize and to keep up appearances of still being *somebody*. Although his acting career spanned seventy years, he is best remembered as the Fernwood Flasher in the 1970s

TV series *Mary Hartman, Mary Hartman*. And that's how those who recognized him saw the lonely, old man.

It's believed that Kilian met a man at one of the bars he favored, and invited the stranger home. Once inside the apartment, this person robbed Kilian, bludgeoned him to death—and got away with murder. This is where the ghostly Kilian comes in. He keeps a lonely vigil at the forecourt of the TCL Theater, hoping to right the injustice that befell him and to locate his killer.

Clifton Webb and Suzy

Among other things, my late friend Suzy Dwyer was a ghost hunter, a movie buff, and somewhat of an expert on the silent era. Suzy often visited the Hollywood Forever Cemetery with her boyfriend. We enjoyed many ghost investigations and discussions about the golden age of film from 1920 to 1950. Over an excellent Mexican dinner one night in Tonopah, Nevada, our talk turned to Clifton Webb. After discussing his former haunted house on Rexford Drive in Hollywood, Suzy shared the following story with me.

You've heard about that haunted chair of his? Who would be stupid enough to sit in it and let his ghost slap them? They say he haunts Hollywood Forever; well let me tell you this:

What a strange experience, not ghostly but strange. We were looking for Rudolph Valentino and Clifton Webb . . . I was worried that the place would close before we found either one of them. While we walked, I told my boyfriend about some of the stars buried there. We stopped outside the Abbey of the Psalms. "This is where Clifton Webb is . . . Mr. Belvedere . . . He was so persnickety and had some sort of mama complex or something," I said.

When the walls of the mausoleum start shaking, I wondered what was going on. "Maybe it's the ghost of Clifton Webb," I laughed. But I didn't really believe it. When we went inside the mausoleum it sounded like someone was throwing pebbles at us. The roof is glass. I thought it may have been birds so I looked up. There weren't any. The sound followed us as we walked through. Neither of us could find any reason for it.

We drained our pitcher of strawberry margaritas and decided that the ghostly Clifton Webb had taken offense at Suzy having said he had a mama complex.

Superman Awaits His Cue

There's a reason that realtors in many states are required by law to inform prospective buyers that a death has occurred in a house, particularly if that death was violent or a suicide. There's the strong possibility that a ghost might come along with the house. If the death happened to a celebrity, the likelihood is probably increased. We all know that celebrities aren't wont to walk away from publicity.

June 16, 1959, George Reeves was forty-seven years old and his world was turned upside down. His long-running TV series *Superman* was on hiatus, which essentially meant he was out of work. It happens to actors, but that didn't make it any easier for Reeves. He had become typecast, which is not a good thing for an actor. Whenever he tried out for a new role, all producers saw was Superman.

While his girlfriend and three guests were visiting his home at 1579 Benedict Canyon, the heavy-drinking Reeves went upstairs to his bedroom and shot himself. At least that's what his girlfriend and his guests told investigators. Conveniently, that was also the official finding of the coroner.

Reeves's mother disagreed. Many of Reeves's friends agreed with her; something about the actor's death didn't add up. There were too many unanswered questions, but the coroner didn't waiver. After two autopsies George Reeves was cremated and his ashes laid to rest in a crypt at Sunrise Corridor at Mountain View Cemetery in Altadena.

Eventually new people moved into the little house on Benedict Canyon and the world moved on. But the restless ghost of George Reeves didn't. The unusual activity started with the sound of gunshots that rang out around three in the morning, the same time that Reeves supposedly shot himself. After failing to find a logical reason for the noise, residents wondered if George Reeves might be trying to reach out from the grave. When the ghostly Reeves appeared in the living room dressed in his Superman costume and smiling broadly, they had their answer. Apparently, the actor was not resting peacefully. This was enough to convince them to pack up and move out.

Since then numerous people have lived in the Superman house. Many of them report having encountered either the ghostly Reeves himself in his old bedroom or out on the front lawn. Most of the time he appears in his Superman costume, his cape rippling in the ghostly breeze. George Reeves is not the only ghost in residence. And those who've encountered this other ghost say he, or she, is negative and unfriendly.

Those who believe that George Reeves was the victim of foul play point to the haunting as proof. The ghostly Reeves, they say, stays on seeking justice for his untimely death and the fact that someone got away with his murder.

Peg's at the Hollywood Sign

> I am afraid, I am a coward. I am sorry for everything.
> If I had done this a long time ago, it would have
> saved a lot of pain.
>
> —Peg Entwistle's suicide note

It's one of Hollywood's oldest ghost stories—and its most enduring. Anyone who saw Netflix's delightful miniseries *Hollywood* is somewhat familiar with the story of Peg Entwistle. Young, talented woman comes to Hollywood from faraway, wanting nothing more than a shot at stardom and all its trappings; the theme is as much a part of Hollywood lore as the tale of actress Lana Turner being discovered at Schwab's while sucking down a soda. She wasn't. Nonetheless it satisfies the public's notion than anyone with the looks and the luck can be a star.

The aforementioned Lana Turner was an eleven-year-old girl the night Peg Entwistle decided her life was no longer worth living. Early in the evening of September 16, 1932, Peg dressed neatly, checked her lipstick, and told her uncle she was going to visit friends. She was young; he thought nothing about it. But Peg had other ideas. The twenty-four-year-old actress was despondent over the direction her acting career was taking. Rather than the serious roles she longed for, Entwistle was being given nothing but comedic roles. She hastily wrote her suicide note, stuffed it in her pocket, and walked to the southern slope of Mount Lee and the fifty-foot-tall Hollywoodland sign. In another seventeen years the sign would be shortened to simply Hollywood. This wouldn't matter to Peg Entwistle. She took off her coat, dropped her purse, and slowly climbed up a workman's ladder to the letter H.

Once on top, she may have stopped long enough to gaze up at the crescent moon and then down at the twinkling lights of the city.

She was sure that there was nothing left for her. Perhaps she simply got to the top and jumped off. Either way, Peg Entwistle was dead the minute she hit the ground. Her body was discovered two days later by a woman walking in the area. And the rumors began. So did the ghost sightings. Peg Entwistle hadn't figured on the fact that she might not be leaving this world as easily as she imagined.

Countless Griffith Park employees have reported seeing a forlorn woman wandering aimlessly in the area where Peg Entwistle made her jump. Her clothing is from another era and she seems to be confused and unhappy. If she is approached the ghostly Peg quickly vanishes. However, Peg Entwistle's favorite fragrance, gardenias, hangs in the air long afterward.

Here I'll share what my late friend Suzy Dwyer said about her Peg experience.

> We went to up to Mount Lee on a whim. The sort of gloomy, gray day that makes you think of *Dark Shadows*. The trail up isn't so bad. We were almost to the back of Hollywood and were making our way to the H when we heard someone whimpering. Not crying, not moaning, but whimpering. I said, "Peg, is that you? Are you here?"
>
> The whimpering stopped. I knew it was her. We looked all around but we didn't see anyone, not living or dead. "Listen Peg," I said. "You don't have to stay here if you don't want to."
>
> I know they say you can't send ghosts to the light; I said it anyway. All of a sudden we felt a rush of cold air blowing across us like someone was fanning us. My boyfriend said it was the wind and I was only imagining things. But trust me, it was Peg Entwistle. I am certain.

Ozzie's Misadventures

It was a 1950s black-and-white television staple, the *Adventures of Ozzie and Harriet,* an early-day sitcom that also starred the real-life couple's sons, David and Ricky. The Nelsons seemed to be the all-American family: Ozzie was the all-wise dad, while harried Harriet kept house and prepared the family meals. The successful show ran from 1952 to 1966. In that time Ricky Nelson became a heartthrob rock and roll star and David a producer/director.

The family home was located at 1822 Camino Palmero Street in the Las Colinas Heights area of Los Angeles. Harriet, Ozzie, David, and Ricky have long since passed on; they haven't resided in the Camino Palmero home for several decades. And yet—it's said that the ghostly Ozzie is still in residence. Ozzie died in one of the bedrooms. Perhaps his ghost isn't even aware of this occurrence. Lights turn on and off, and there is the occasional aroma of rose perfume (although this doesn't seem like a fragrance Ozzie might favor).

According to the ladies, Ozzie is the type of ghost who hasn't a clue as to twenty-first-century rules regarding sexual harassment. He occasionally touches women inappropriately or kisses them on the neck. That doesn't sound like the all-wise dad of television from back in the day. But those who've encountered the ghostly Ozzie say it's true. He can't keep his hands to himself. All we can hope is that Harriet will one day make an appearance and take Ozzie in hand.

Hot Toddy

*B*londe and beautiful, immensely talented, Thelma Todd was known as Hot Toddy to some and the Ice Cream Blonde to others. The actress rose to stardom in the silent era of the 1920s. Unlike some actresses who saw their careers falter and fail with the advent of sound, Thelma Todd's career continued to skyrocket right up until the night of her mysterious death.

December 15, 1935, was a cold night across Southern California. In Hollywood, Thelma had been invited to a birthday bash at the popular Trocadero nightclub. Once there, she partied with friends until the early morning hours; feeling woozy, she called her chauffeur to drive her home to her apartment over her café at 17535 Pacific Coast Highway.

It's believed that Thelma Todd had somehow locked herself out of her apartment that night. She knocked on the door. Unable to wake her fiancée/business partner, Roland West, who slept in his apartment next to hers, Todd crept down the stairs toward her garage. An icy wind swept in from the ocean intensifying the chill that hung in the air. She hugged her fur coat tightly against the cold, as she made her way to her car, which was parked in the garage. She crawled into the front seat and pulled the fur tighter. Even so, she was still cold. In her effort to stay warm, Thelma Todd made a fatal decision. She turned on the car's engine and heater. She'd had a lot to drink and quickly fell asleep.

While she slept, Thelma Todd was overcome by carbon monoxide fumes and died there in the garage. Her death would become a Hollywood legend—the unsolved death of a star like the Ice Cream Blonde captured the public's attention much as that of Marilyn Monroe would decades later.

What happened to Thelma Todd in the time between her leaving the party and her body being discovered is open to speculation. It's possible that her chauffeur lied about how and when Thelma Todd arrived home. But why? Did a killer accompany her to the garage? Or was someone waiting for her in the garage? Was she beaten unconscious and placed in the car? These are questions that likely will never be answered. We do know that when her maid discovered Todd's body the next day, it was apparent the death was no suicide. Rumor held that Thelma Todd had suffered bruises and broken ribs. Clearly, someone had assaulted the actress. Even so, the coroner's jury found that the death was accidental. Much has been written about Thelma Todd's death. But the question remains: Was the death a suicide, an accident, or murder? That depends on whose book you read.

The ghostly Thelma Todd is sometimes seen at the top of the stairs where her apartment once was. She's also been spotted in and around the building that once housed her Thelma Todd's Sidewalk Café, as well as the garage where she died. Some say they've heard a car running in the garage even when no car is parked there. Others say they've detected the odor of carbon monoxide in the empty garage. Perhaps the ghostly starlet is hoping that the truth of her long-ago death will someday be revealed.

Harlow's Haunted Hideaway

*T*he story of Jean Harlow is yet another Hollywood tale that proves beauty and talent are not enough to keep tragedy at bay. A box office draw, Harlow made over thirty movies from 1927 to 1937, and if not for her untimely death at age twenty-six, Jean Harlow would have outshone Hollywood's biggest female names. She didn't get the chance. She died of renal failure on June 7, 1937.

The home she shared with her husband, Paul Bern, on Easton Drive, off Benedict Canyon Drive, is said to be haunted by Jean Harlow and Paul Bern. They married in July 1932. Two months later Bern was found shot to death in Harlow's bedroom. A suicide note read:

> Dearest Dear,
> Unfortunately this is the only way to make good the frightful wrong I have done you and to wipe out my abject humiliation.
> > I love you.
> > Paul
> > You understand that last night was only a comedy.

The distraught bride claimed to know nothing. Rather than call the cops, Jean's assistants called the studio heads. They would make sure that no hint of scandal touched their platinum moneymaker. Eventually the police were called and the investigation began.

During the investigation it was discovered that Bern had been married once before—and he hadn't bothered to get a divorce. Suspicion fell on this first wife, who killed herself before police could question her. A rumor has persisted that Jean Harlow shot Paul Bern in retaliation for a terrible beating he'd given her. The official verdict was suicide and the case was closed, just another Hollywood scandal neatly wrapped up.

Jean Harlow moved out of the house after Bern's death. She would only live another five years herself; in that time she never spoke about Bern's death publicly. Both Bern and Harlow are rumored to haunt the house. The most famous sighting of the ghostly Paul Bern was by that of murder victim Sharon Tate. Her boyfriend Jay Sebring, who owned the home, was away at the time. She was alone in the house's master bedroom when she was startled by the appearance of what she called a creepy little man. He walked into the bedroom and looked through the dresser drawers as if he was searching for something. Realizing he was a ghost, the frightened actress ran down the stairs to escape the apparition. At the bottom of the stairs, she saw the vision of a blonde woman tied to the bannister, her throat slit and blood everywhere.

A horrible dream she just couldn't shake, or was it something more? Some believe it was a foretelling of what the future held for her and Jay Sebring.

The ghostly Harlow occasionally appears in the downstairs bedroom. A transparent figure, her platinum blonde hair gleaming, she quietly moves about the room then slowly vanishes.

Sam Kinison Challenges a Ghost at the Comedy Store

*D*on't go down in the basement. According to some former employees this is where the worst ghostly activity seems to be centered at the Comedy Store on Sunset Strip. When it opened its doors on January 29, 1940, the building was Ciro's, a popular Hollywood hot spot. Lana Turner claimed it was her favorite nightclub.

This could be because Ciro's owner, Billy Wilkerson, was the man who discovered Lana when she was Julia Jean Turner, a fifteen-year-old high school student, skipping class at the Top Hat Malt Shop. Then again perhaps it was because Ciro's was the place to see and be seen for the publicity-craving Hollywood set. Marilyn Monroe, Betty Grable, Humphrey Bogart, James Stewart, Peter Lawford, and Judy Garland are just a few names from a long list of stars that frequented Ciro's.

Movie stars weren't the only people impressed with Ciro's. Gangsters like blue-eyed Bugsy Siegel and Johnny Roselli were regulars as well. Roselli, it was rumored, took part in Wilkerson's high-stakes card games. Incidentally, both Siegel and Roselli ended up on the wrong side of a mob hit. Long before their unfortunate ends, their cohorts were rumored to have tortured, beaten, and possibly killed any number of people who were slow in paying their gambling debts in the basement of Ciro's. And this could be why the negative energy and ghosts are reported here still.

In 1972 Ciro's was transformed into the Comedy Store with new owners and new ideas. Here would be a place for stand-up comics. Those just starting out could try their stuff in front of real audiences. Richard Pryor, Jim Carrey, Whoopi Goldberg, Jay Leno, and Robin Williams are some who got their start at the comedy club. Into the mix came loudmouthed Sam Kinison, a former Pentecostal preacher with a penchant for routines that sometimes centered on misogyny and homophobia. During a routine in which he endured the usual problems with sound equipment and lights, Sam Kinison challenged the ghosts of the Comedy Store.

Yelling out a taunting remark to the ghost, Kinison waited for an apparition to appear on stage with him. That didn't happen. Instead, every light in the house went off. Kinison and patrons sat in darkness for a minute before the lights came up again.

Numerous people, employees and patrons alike, have reported their ghostly experiences at the Comedy Store. In her book *Hollywood Haunted*, author Laurie Jacobson details some experiences during the time she worked there as a cocktail waitress in the early 1980s.

In 1990, two years before his death, Kinison publicly disavowed his former ways, and helped to raise a half million dollars for the research and fight against AIDS. He seemed to realize how wrong and hurtful his jokes were and he may have even mellowed with time. That opportunity ended with a head-on collision on April 10, 1992. Kinison's white Trans Am was struck by a drunk driver's truck on US Route 95 fifteen miles outside of Needles. The mystery that will forever surround his death—who was Sam Kinison talking to as he died?

A witness reported that Kinison said, "I don't want to die. I don't want to die."

He listened briefly then asked, "But why?"

After receiving his answer, the critically injured comedian sighed, "Okay, okay, okay."

Then he was gone.

Marilyn

Like Rudolph Valentino, the ghostly Marilyn Monroe is everywhere, making her one of the busiest ghosts in Hollywood. This could be because so much mystery surrounds her last days. The cause of her August 5, 1962, death at age thirty-six is still debated. Was it murder, or was it suicide?

It was well known that Marilyn Monroe had issues and used drugs. Her life was a train wreck. She'd recently gone through a divorce with playwright Arthur Miller and reportedly attempted suicide at Frank Sinatra's Cal Neva Lodge, only to be revived and flown back to Los Angeles and the fate that awaited her. Not so well known at the time were her affairs with President Kennedy and his brother Robert.

Also not known to her adoring public were Monroe's threats to release her little book in which she kept names, dates, and details. In the 1960s this would have spelled doom with a capital D to the careers of both Kennedys. Was she silenced for this reason? Her little book has never turned up. And likely it never will. There are more books about Marilyn Monroe and the lurid details of her death than there are cosmetic surgeons in Beverly Hills. And they will continue to be written. But without the crucial evidence of what took place that night at 12305 Fifth Helena Drive, they are theories. This may be why the ghost of Marilyn Monroe continues to hang around in Hollywood and other locations.

As previously discussed, there is that haunted Marilyn Monroe mirror at the Hollywood Roosevelt Hotel. It is also rumored that Marilyn has appeared lounging by the swimming pool and at other spots throughout her former home on Fifth Helena Drive. This would make sense if she was murdered and thus unaware of her own demise.

Dispensing with that theory is the many sightings of Marilyn at her crypt at Westwood Memorial Park. Ethereal and still beautiful, the ghostly Marilyn knows that she is no longer of this world. But she is pleased to be remembered by the many fans that stop to pay her homage. Marilyn has also been spotted at her star on the Hollywood Walk of Fame. She seems to enjoy the fact that her fame is enduring.

Beverly Hills Hotel

*T*he Pink Palace, so called for the shade of pink that covers its exterior walls, is a luxurious hotel that's been favored by world leaders and celebrities since it opened in 1912. According to Hollywood legend, a lot of lurid history that didn't make it into the days' newspapers was played out at the Beverly Hills Hotel.

The tony hotel's bungalows are very private and secluded. While campaigning for the presidency in 1960, John F. Kennedy kept a bungalow at the hotel where he met and entertained starlets of the day. Future first lady Jackie was none the wiser. Marilyn Monroe and Yves Montand had a romantic fling or two in Bungalows 20 and 21. Howard Hughes spent time in one of the bungalows as did Vivien Leigh and Laurence Olivier.

Because they are hidden, the bungalows are very popular. And at least three guests have chosen to stay on at the Beverly Hills Hotel: Peter Finch, Sergei Rachmaninoff, and Harpo Marx haunt bungalows on the property.

On January 14, 1977, sixty-year-old actor Peter Finch was relaxing in the lobby of the Beverly Hills Hotel when he was suddenly struck with a massive heart attack and died there in the lobby. He was nominated for a best actor award for his role in *Network*, and is only one of two actors who have received a posthumous best actor Oscar.

Russian composer Sergei Rachmaninoff and comedian Harpo Marx lived with their families in Beverly Hills. Perhaps they had clandestine meetings with secret lovers in bungalows. And the memories of those happier days are why the two men have chosen to stay on and haunt bungalows at the Beverly Hills Hotel. Doubtful they could find a more elegant place to haunt.

Valentino

*R*udolph Valentino was at the zenith of his career when he died of peritonitis at age thirty-one on August 23, 1926. Apparently, the Latin Lover didn't like being dead. His ex-wife, Natacha Rambova, claimed that the ghostly Valentino came and talked with her often. Although he'd met and liked the great tenor Enrique Caruso in the afterlife, he was not happy and didn't think he was receiving enough respect since his death. What's more, he didn't think that death should be any reason that he could not write the script for a movie he'd been contemplating.

For this purpose, the ghostly Valentino contacted Mrs. Carol E. McKinstry, a spiritual medium who later wrote a book about her experiences with Valentino from the great beyond titled *The Return of Rudolph Valentino.*

When he wasn't contacting mediums or his former wife, the ghostly Valentino began haunting several locations. He has been seen around his crypt in the Cathedral Mausoleum at the Hollywood Forever Cemetery. It is believed that he doesn't rest in peace because an adequate memorial, though planned and talked about, was not erected in his honor.

The ghostly Rudy has also been seen at numerous Southern California locations, including the Santa Maria Inn in Santa Maria. He prefers Room 221 and has been known to knock on the door until it is opened. Then he makes a grand entrance and plops down on the bed. Occasionally Valentino is spotted on the veranda of an old beach house, or at the location of his former home, Falcon Lair. A dog lover, Valentino is usually accompanied by two of his beloved pets.

It's rumored that Valentino's untimely death was brought on by a cursed ring he bought at a jewelry store in San Francisco in 1921. When his eyes fell on a stunning cat's eye ring, he had to have it.

The shop owner warned him that the ring was cursed. But Valentino scoffed at the superstitious idea. How could he believe in such nonsense when thus far life had gone his way? No simple ring could change that. He was Rudolph Valentino, star of the silver screen; he was used to having what he wanted. He stubbornly bought the ring and slipped it on his finger. He wore it while filming *The Young Rajah* in 1922. The film flopped. Was it the ring's curse or the strangely lavish costumes, designed by Natacha Rambova (Mrs. Valentino), that contributed to the movie's failure?

Rudolph Valentino didn't know Mrs. Evalyn Walsh McLean, the last private owner of the brilliant blue Hope Diamond, who could have warned him about the bad luck cursed jewelry can bring. So could the Hope Diamond's former owners French King Louis XVI and his wife, Marie Antoinette, who kept their appointment with the guillotine.

Valentino would make five more films in the next three years. None would be the loser that *The Young Rajah* was. Could that be because Rudolph Valentino was not wearing his cursed ring in those other films? *The Son of the Sheik* would be his last film. When filming wrapped up, he traveled to New York for publicity. And he wore the ring.

During his New York tour, Valentino collapsed and was hospitalized. After surgery for appendicitis and gastric ulcers, his condition worsened. He died eight days later. Valentino was just one of many who were closely associated with the ring that would suffer untimely death. Some say the ring is safely locked away in a vault somewhere; others say it is lost forever, its whereabouts unknown for decades. Since no one knows exactly where it is, the ghostly Valentino wanders various locations throughout Beverly Hills and the Hollywood Forever Cemetery looking for his lost ring.

Knickerbocker Hotel, Calling Harry Houdini

*T*oday the Hollywood Knickerbocker Hotel is known as the Hollywood Knickerbocker Apartments, a senior community of studio and one-bedroom apartments. Since it first opened in June 1929, the hotel attracted many of Hollywood's glamorous elite. Marilyn Monroe and Joe DiMaggio often shared drinks at the hotel's bar. While filming *Love Me Tender*, Elvis Presley stayed in Room 1016. Jerry Lee Lewis, Lana Turner, Frank Sinatra, Johnny Mercer, and Mae West are stars who were guests at the hotel.

There is also a dark side. The Knickerbocker was the site of filmmaker D. W. Griffith's death in the lounge; likewise actor William Frawley passed in the lounge of the Knickerbocker. But it was the Halloween 1936 séance of Harry Houdini's wife, Bess Houdini, on the rooftop of the Knickerbocker that brought its most famous paranormal happening.

For ten years Bess Houdini had held a séance on the anniversary of her husband's death, hoping that he would come through the veil and talk with her. It was an unusually cold night in Los Angeles as a crowd of eager participants gathered at the Knickerbocker Hotel. A tambourine, a trumpet, a bell, chalk, and a chalkboard were placed on the table awaiting the ghostly Harry Houdini to come from the afterlife. And the séance began.

"Please Harry, I've been waiting so long," Bess Houdini coaxed.

Houdini didn't make an appearance. Nor did he acknowledge Bess or the others who tried to communicate with him. Later Bess Houdini would say,

"Houdini did not come through. My last hope is gone. I do not believe that Houdini can come back to me, or to anyone . . . The Houdini Shrine has burned for ten years. I now, reverently . . . turn out the light. It is finished. Good night, Harry!"

Apparently, Harry Houdini doesn't haunt the Hollywood Knickerbocker Hotel. This doesn't mean the building is devoid of ghosts. The specter most often witnessed is the ghostly bellhop who's been spotted on every floor. Apparently, he keeps things in order for the hotel's afterlife clients. This is Hollywood, and a few movie stars are bound to want to stay on indefinitely.

The tragic film star Frances Farmer, who was hauled out of her hotel room naked by police officers on January 14, 1943, is thought to haunt the Knickerbocker to this day. She is responsible for the cold spots that are felt in certain areas of the building and the sobbing that is heard in the hallways in the early morning hours.

Marilyn Monroe is said to hang out in one of the ladies' bathrooms. Exactly why the blonde star would choose to do so is a mystery in itself. Silent screen star Rudolph Valentino supposedly haunts the Knickerbocker; admittedly, this seems strange considering that he was dead three years before the place was even built.

Chateau Marmont

Luxurious, legendary—and haunted—that's the Chateau Marmont. An often-told legend is that the Chateau Marmont was the inspiration for the Eagles' 1977 hit "Hotel California." True or not, the hotel was built in 1927 for the moneyed Hollywood set who enjoyed their excesses while demanding privacy and elegance. A-listers who've stayed here include Howard Hughes, Greta Garbo, and John Belushi. Belushi is one who has decided to stay on indefinitely.

Belushi was young and talented. His career was soaring, but he had a problem with drugs. Shortly after midnight on March 5, 1982, he was found dead in his bungalow at the Chateau Marmont. The combination of heroin and cocaine, known as a speedball, was his doom. Apparently, he regrets his death and still feels a connection to our world. Some who've stayed in Bungalow 3 have encountered the ghostly comedian. He isn't trying to scare people, but rather trying to entertain them with his ghostly antics—once an entertainer, always an entertainer.

Also rumored to be in residence is the ghostly actor Boris Karloff, who stayed at the Chateau Marmont often. Karloff, who portrayed Frankenstein on screen, is responsible for the lights turning on and off as well as water faucets that turn on after being turned off. Some guests claim to have awakened in the middle of the night to see his disembodied head floating above their bed. Yes, that's creepy. But then, that's Karloff for you.

The Chateau Marmont guards its guests' privacy. Only guests are permitted on the property. Wherever you're staying on the property, no one living will bother you—ghosts, however, are a different matter.

Thomas Ince Wants His Office

*L*ike so many Hollywood deaths, Thomas Ince's death is shrouded in mystery. Known as the Father of the Western, the successful film producer and studio owner had just turned forty-two when he boarded William Randolph Hearst's opulent 280-foot yacht, the *Oneida*, on November 16, 1924. The two men were involved in negotiations and planned on discussing business and then celebrating Ince's birthday. Among the guests onboard were gossip columnist Louella Parsons, actor Charlie Chaplin, writer Elinor Glyn, and Marion Davies, Hearst's lady love.

The next day, Ince was gravely ill. He was taken from the *Oneida* on a stretcher to an awaiting train and taken home where he died. The *Oneida*'s doctor said Ince had a peptic ulcer and had become violently ill after a night of drinking champagne and eating salted almonds. Charlie Chaplin's secretary would later say that Ince had a head wound that was bleeding when he was moved from the *Oneida*.

Strangely, the *Los Angeles Times* carried a story titled "Movie Producer shot in head on yacht." Hearst had money, which meant he had clout. The story was never printed or discussed again. The rumors didn't stop. People speculated that, knowing that Charlie Chaplin and Marion Davies were carrying on an affair, Hearst waited for his opportunity to shoot Chaplin. The only problem was that he had shot Ince by mistake.

Whatever the truth, Thomas Ince's wife had a new trust fund thanks to William Randolph Hearst. So she went along with the peptic ulcer story. Louella Parsons had a guaranteed job for life with Hearst publications, so she agreed to maintain her silence as well. The stories were quashed as fast as they appeared. Just to make certain there would be no future questions or exhumations, Thomas

Ince was quickly—and quietly—cremated, and his ashes scattered at sea.

If there is truth to the rumors, Ince was betrayed by just about everyone he knew. This kind of injustice can make for an angry and restless ghost. Maybe this is the reason those who work in Thomas Ince's old office building at Culver Studios in Culver City claim to see him. Ince's grim-faced apparition has also been spotted walking up and down the stairs that lead to his office and in the old stage area. Remodeling is one sure way to stir up ghostly activity. Apparently, Thomas Ince was not pleased with all the changes that had taken place.

The ghostly Ince made his displeasure obvious one afternoon when he angrily appeared before workers, announcing, "I don't like what you're doing to my studio!"

The frightened men picked up their tools and left for the day.

Errol Flynn's Farm

From his first Hollywood starring role in the 1935 *Captain Blood,* Errol Flynn shot to stardom. As Hollywood's leading man in the 1930s through the early 1940s, the actor was in high demand. But there was a dark side to Errol Flynn. He was a heavy drinker who partied too much. In 1942 his antics caught up with him when he found himself in the middle of a lurid scandal. Two teenage girls accused him of statutory rape while aboard his first yacht, *Sirocco.* With well-known Hollywood attorney Jerry Geisler acting as his defense attorney, Flynn was easily acquitted of the charges.

He was free, but his career took a big hit. He would do more films but he would lose standing and would never again achieve what he once had. He was Errol Flynn and he liked flouting society's rules.

While visiting Vancouver, British Columbia, with his seventeen-year-old girlfriend, Flynn died on the night of October 15, 1959. Twelve hundred miles away at his Mulholland Farm, Flynn's house shook at the exact moment of his death. Did this signal the return of the ghostly Flynn to his beloved home? Anyone who knew him well knew that Errol Flynn's home was no ordinary home, haunted or not. Flynn had secret passageways, staircases, and two-way mirrors included in his home when he had it built. While there was paranormal activity from the moment Flynn died, it intensified after former teen heartthrob Ricky Nelson, a fan of Errol Flynn, purchased the home in 1980.

While living at Mulholland Farm, Nelson and his family experienced plenty of ghostly activity. Errol Flynn himself was seen on occasion in an upstairs bedroom. He always appeared in a tuxedo. He was not alone. Throughout the house other apparitions appeared.

Faucets turning on and off, lights flickering, noises like breaking glass and furniture banging up against the walls, and the overwhelming flowery odor of a woman's perfume were all common occurrences. None of this seemed to bother Ricky Nelson, who felt a kinship with Flynn. But the otherworldly activity set his family's nerves on edge.

In 2011 Nelson's daughter, Tracy, appeared on an episode of the TV show *My Celebrity Ghost Story* to tell about her experience living in the house. She painted a macabre picture of what it was like living in the darkly haunted Mulholland Farm.

Ricky Nelson was killed in a fiery plane crash in Texas on December 31, 1985. After his death the hauntings at Flynn's former Mulholland Farm became worse. The family moved out and the house stood empty for many years. Since then the house has been razed and the property divided into smaller lots. Other houses were built and other families moved in. Does the ghost of Errol Flynn still walk the property where his home once stood?

Boris Karloff's Haunted Rose Garden

*T*he average gardener would probably be horrified if a friend asked to have his or her cremains scattered in their garden, but horror actor Boris Karloff was not your average gardener.

According to one story, Katharine Hepburn used to live in the house and was convinced the place was haunted. Karloff bought his home and acreage from her. Ghosts didn't frighten Karloff, who became famous and wealthy playing the monster Frankenstein on the screen.

In 1938 he and his wife moved into their new home, and Karloff set to work creating a magnificent garden oasis. Karloff's garden so impressed his friends that many of them asked to have their cremains scattered among the roses.

Legend has it that Karloff, whose real name was William Henry Pratt, obliged some of them. And that, they say, may be the reason the rose garden is haunted. The ghosts who reside in the garden are said to be pleasant and content. What better place to have perspective than a garden? Oddly, the ghostly Katharine Hepburn has made an appearance at the garden. Surely, she's overcome her fear of ghosts having become one herself.

Boris Karloff moved out when he and his wife divorced in 1946. Over the years other people have moved in, and moved out, because of the ghosts. The garden and the ghosts remain to this day. Although he is said to haunt other locations, one of the rose garden's ghostly residents is said to be none other than Boris Karloff himself.

At this writing, new owners have purchased the charming home on Bowmont Drive.

Dracula's in the Building

To movie fans the world over, Bela Lugosi was Dracula. The 1931 film *Dracula* was the first horror film with sound. The role made him a star—and a legend. When the cameras weren't rolling, Lugosi lived a tortured life. He was addicted to morphine, and happiness seemed to elude him. He was married and divorced four times. His fifth and last marriage ended with his death of a heart attack.

According to a story that came out two years before the film *Dracula*, a young Béla Ferenc Dezső Blaskó (Bela Lugosi) met a mysterious woman with yellow eyes in his native Hungary. He wasn't sure himself if she was a ghost, a demon, or merely an ordinary woman who held a strange power over him. But she did indeed hold power over him. According to some, she would haunt him throughout his life.

Broke, typecast, sick, forgotten, and out of work, Bela Lugosi died in his Hollywood apartment on August 16, 1956, yet his ghost seems to have overlooked that fact. Lugosi was buried wearing his Dracula costume and cape at the Holy Cross Cemetery in Culver City and has since been seen countless times in his old apartment. He looks like a living person—right up to the time he walks through the wall. And if you're curious, yes, he is wearing his cape and Dracula makeup.

Jayne Mansfield's Haunted Pink Palace

*H*oping to break into the movies, busty blonde bombshell Jayne Mansfield came to Hollywood in the early 1950s with husband Paul Mansfield and her child in tow. Five years later the Marilyn Monroe copycat was a *Playboy* magazine centerfold. Although she achieved celebrity status, she didn't achieve the stardom she'd hoped for. In 1958 she divorced Mansfield and married Mr. Universe Mickey Hargitay. Together they moved into Jayne's forty-room mansion on Sunset Boulevard in Holmby Hills. They remade the house into what would become known as the Pink Palace. Pink was the central color: pink exterior walls, pink florescent lights, a pink bathtub, pink fixtures, pink furnishings, and a pink heart-shaped swimming pool. Completing the pink pretention was a fountain that was said to gurgle pink champagne.

Three kids and six years later, the Hargitays divorced. As her career faltered and her popularity waned, Jayne Mansfield was forced to take work where she could find it: Vegas showrooms and small second-rate nightclubs. And then in 1966, at a film festival in San Francisco, she met Anton LaVey, the founder of the First Church of Satan. A fast friendship formed between the two, much to the dismay of Mansfield's attorney-boyfriend Sam Brody.

From the start, Brody and LaVey intensely disliked each other. Jealous of the time Jayne and LaVey were spending together at Jayne's Pink Palace and LaVey's black house in San Francisco, Brody got into an argument with LaVey, telling him to leave her alone. LaVey retaliated by angrily placing a curse on Brody, telling him that he would be dead within the year. LaVey then turned to Jayne and warned her not to ride in a car with Brody. She didn't heed his advice. They'd been in seven car accidents together. In the early morning hours of June 29, 1967, they were killed, along with their driver, in a horrific car accident on a Mississippi back road. Jayne's children, who were asleep in the backseat, survived.

After her death, Jayne's Pink Palace was sold. New owners moved in—and moved out. Apparently, the ghostly Jayne had returned to her beloved Pink Palace. One of the new owners reported hearing a woman's voice softly coaxing, "Get out!"

There was the fragrance of Jayne's favorite perfume that would suddenly drift through the air. And the ghostly Jayne herself would occasionally appear before startled witnesses.

Ringo Starr was another owner. He decided against the garish pink and had the exterior walls repainted white. It would take several coats of paint to keep the pink from seeping through.

In 1976 Engelbert Humperdinck bought the house and moved in. In 2002 Humperdinck sold the Pink Palace to developers. The mansion was razed that same year.

Elke Sommer and the Ghost

*D*uring the late 1960s the haunted Hollywood home of actress Elke Sommer and her husband, well-known Hollywood writer Joe Hyams, was covered in magazines such as *Fate* magazine and the *Saturday Evening Post*. Hyams also wrote a book about their haunted abode titled *The Day I Gave up the Ghost*.

It started when a friend noticed a man staring at her from the dining room. There was no man in the house at the time. It didn't take long for the Hyams to realize they had a ghost in residence. After being awakened night after night by noises that sounded like their dining room chairs were being scraped along the floor and a noisy party was going on in their home, they called the American Society for Psychical Research (ASPR) for help. They conducted several séances in the house on Benedict Canyon in an effort to learn more about who was haunting the house and why.

The cameraman who came with the ASPR claimed that something had happened to a roll of film in his camera that convinced him there was paranormal activity going on. The Hyams moved out one night, never to return after an entity knocked at their bedroom door alerting them that there was a fire in the house. What if there had been no knock? The fire had been very real, too close, and very dangerous. Enough was enough. Legend has it the home was sold seventeen more times because of the ghostly man in the tuxedo who haunts the place.

Lon Chaney and Frank Stites Just Hanging Out at Universal Studios

Silent film star Lon Chaney, the man of a thousand faces, gave masterful performances as twisted characters. With his makeup kit Chaney skillfully transformed himself into any character a role required. He rose to stardom playing Quasimodo in the 1923 film *Hunchback of Notre Dame*, which grossed three and a half million dollars for Universal, making it the studio's most successful silent film. Two years later he starred in *The Phantom of the Opera*, another hit for Universal and Chaney.

Soundstage 28, one of the first stages built on the lot, was created especially for *The Phantom of the Opera* set. Lon Chaney would make fifteen more films for Universal before his untimely death of lung cancer in 1930 at the age of forty-seven. There were those who believed that Lon Chaney never left Soundstage 28, and that his ghost continued to haunt the site of his most famous film. Decked out in his cape, the ghostly Chaney was seen dozens of times on the soundstage or running across the catwalks.

Footsteps, slamming doors, lights that turned off and on, and whispered conversations were reported by employees who worked inside the building when the studio was deserted. Those who didn't believe the stories of the ghostly Chaney were convinced after they'd encountered him themselves. Chaney never said a word, or acknowledged stunned onlookers as he rushed past them.

Another Hollywood legend concerning the ghostly Lon Chaney involves a bus bench on the northwest corner of Hollywood and Vine. Shortly after his death, Lon Chaney was spotted sitting on the bench.

In October 1942 Los Angeles councilman Norris Nelson told a council meeting about the ghostly Chaney and his ornamental iron bus bench. According to Norris, Chaney waited on the bus bench before he became a star. After he was famous, Chaney drove by the bench and often gave extras and others in the film industry a ride to work. The ghostly Lon Chaney and his bench were becoming famous when someone removed it, replacing it with a garish one.

"No self-respecting ghost would sit on such a bench," Nelson told the council.

The bench was not returned and Lon Chaney's ghost was never seen sitting on the new one.

Soundstage 28 was demolished on September 23, 2014. If the ghost of Lon Chaney is still at Universal Studios, he has found a new location to hang out. Perhaps he has chosen the back lot where ghostly actor Frank Stites is said to be.

On March 16, 1915—just two days after famed daredevil aviator Lincoln Beachey died when his plane crashed into the San Francisco Bay at the Panama-Pacific International Exposition—Universal Studios was celebrating the opening of Universal City. It had only been twelve years since Orville and Wilbur Wright flew a plane for the first time at Kitty Hawk, and the public was excited and curious about flight.

As part of the festivities, Los Angeles aviator and stunt pilot Frank Stites was flying a biplane in a mock battle with a dummy plane. As the crowd watched transfixed, something went wrong; the dummy plane exploded and Stites either fell out of his plane or jumped. The plane crashed and Stites fell two hundred feet to the ground.

Later it was said that just before climbing into his biplane, Stites had mentioned Lincoln Beachey's death, saying that he would be the next to die. Sadly, his premonition proved correct.

Like Lon Chaney, the ghostly Frank Stites is said to have stayed on at Universal. Stites prefers to roam the back lot and is believed to be the ghostly man who's been seen dozens of times in the area dressed in aviator gear and goggles from a century ago.

Hollywood Hereafter at Hollywood Forever

It's said that cemeteries are not all that haunted. That might be so in most places, but this is Hollywood, and Hollywood is different. No star wants to lose the attention and adulation of millions of adoring fans—even after death. And this could be why so many celebrities continue to stay here even after death has claimed them.

Hollywood Forever was founded in 1899 and was listed on the National Register of Historic Places a century later in 1999. The cemetery is called the "resting place of Hollywood's immortals." And it truly is. Some may be resting more peacefully than others.

Located at 6000 Santa Monica Boulevard, Hollywood Forever is not the hereafter home of Jayne Mansfield, although there is a cenotaph here in her honor. Silent screen actor Douglas Fairbanks, old-time heartthrob Rudolph Valentino, and Darla Hood of the old *Our Gang/Little Rascals* are here. Another member of the cast, Carl "Alfalfa" Switzer, rests nearby. Switzer died at thirty-two when he pulled a knife on the wrong man over a fifty-dollar dispute.

Yet another resident who didn't live to collect a pension is mobster Benjamin "Bugsy" Siegel. Bugsy's at the Beth Olam Mausoleum. Mwaaaaah! A ladies' man in life, so he is in death; just look at all those lipstick kisses on his marker.

A ghostly woman in black has been seen near Rudolph Valentino's crypt in the Cathedral Mausoleum. Most likely she is Ditka Flame, the mysterious woman in black who came here to pay homage to him every year on the anniversary of his death. Flame died in 1984 and is buried in San Jacinto.

The unfortunate Virginia Rappe, who died mysteriously at a Labor Day bash thrown by Roscoe Fatty Arbuckle, is buried here at Hollywood Forever. Visitors to the cemetery have reported hearing the sound of sobbing and weeping as they come upon her grave.

Hollywood Forever is one of those rare cemeteries that plans events for the living as well. In fact, Hollywood Forever hosts the largest Dia de Los Muertos celebration in the US, and during the warm summer months Cinespia presents movies that are shown on the wall of the Cathedral Mausoleum. Not everyone is so busy watching the film that they don't see the ghosts flitting about.

Because Paramount Studios is located close to the Hollywood Forever Cemetery, it is said to be one of Hollywood's most haunted studios. Besides the ghosts that call Paramount home, the ghostly residents of the cemetery occasionally make appearances there as well. Perhaps they are simply homesick for the soundstage and the Hollywood world they were once a part of.

Our ghostly excursion into the Golden State concludes here at the Hollywood Forever Cemetery. Before we find our way to the egress, permit me to say it is my fervent hope that you have enjoyed the journey as much as I have.

Bibliography

Books

Anger, Kenneth, *Hollywood Babylon II*

Bell, Horace (Major), *On the Old West Coast*

Blanche, Tony, and Brad Schreiber, *Death in Paradise*

Caldwell, George D., MD, *Ghost Stories of the California Missions and Rhymes of the Gypsy Trail*

Carr, Harry, *Los Angeles City of Dreams*

Chessman, Caryl, *Cell Block 2455*

Clough, Charles W., *San Juan Bautista*

Clune, Brian, *Hollywood Obscura*

Clune, Brian, and Bob Davis, *Haunted Universal Studios*

Dwyer, Jeff, *Ghost Hunter's Guide to Los Angeles*

Friedman, Mel, *California Gold Rush*

Hauck, Dennis William, *The National Directory of Haunted Places*

Holdredge, Helen, *Mammy Pleasant*

Holdredge, Helen, *Mammy Pleasant's Partner*

Holzer, Hans, *America's Haunted Houses*

Hotel Del Coronado Heritage Department (editor), *Beautiful Stranger: The Ghost of Kate Morgan and the Hotel Del Coronado*

Jacobson, Laurie, and Mark Wanamaker, *Hollywood Haunted: A Ghostly Tour of Filmland*

Karpis, Alvin, *On the Rock*

Kashner, Sam, and Nancy Schoenberger, *Hollywood Kryptonite*

Lee, Hector, *Heroes Villains and Ghosts Folklore of Old California*

Mahony, Patrick, *Unsought Visitors*

Marx, S., and J. Vanderveen, *Deadly Illusions: Jean Harlow and the Murder of Paul Bern*

May, Alan M., *The Legend of Kate Morgan*

May, Antoinette, *Haunted Houses and Wandering Ghosts of California*

McGlashan, C. F., History of the Donner Party

Morehouse III, W., *Millennium Biltmore: A Grand Hotel Born of Hollywood Dreams*

Mulholland, John, *Beware Familiar Spirits*

Oberding, Janice, *Haunted Lake Tahoe*

Ogden, Tom, *Haunted Hollywood*

Ogden, Tom, *Haunted Hotels*

Older, Fremont Mrs., *California Missions and their Romances*

Older, Fremont Mrs., *Love Stories of Old California*

Reinstedt, Randall A., *Ghosts and Mystery Along Old Monterey's Path of History*

Reinstedt, Randall A., *Ghosts of the Big Sur Coast*

Schroeder, B., and C. Fogg, *Beverly Hills Confidential*

Senate, Richard, *Ghosts of the California Missions*

Senate, Richard, *Ghosts of the Haunted Coast*

Senate, Richard, *Ghost Stalker's Guide to Haunted California*

Senate, Richard, *Hollywood's Ghosts*

Shillinglaw, Susan, *Carol and John Steinbeck: Portrait of a Marriage*

Shulman, Irving, *Harlow: An Intimate Biography*

Starr, K., *Material Dreams: Southern California through the 1920s*

Steinbeck, Gwen Conger, *My Life with John Steinbeck*

Wall, Rosaline Sharpe, *A Wild Coast and Lonely*

Walska, Ganna, *Always Room at the Top*

Weller, S., *Dancing at Ciro's*

Wing, R. (editor), *The Blue Book of the Screen*

Wlodarski, Robert J., and Anne Nathan Wlodarski, *Haunted Catalina*

Wolfe, Donald H., *The Black Dahlia Files*

Yasuda, Anita, *Haunted Monterey Peninsula*

Magazines

Borderline, January 1964

Coronet, January 1951

Exhibitors Herald, December 6, 1924

Fate, August 1968

Saturday Evening Post, July 2, 1966

Saturday Evening Post, June 3, 1967

Screenland, December 1921

Whisper, February 1956

Newspapers

Bodie Morning News, September 9, 1879

Butte Montana Standard, November 28, 1942

Gasconade Republican, January 30, 1947

Reno Evening Gazette, February 27, 1882

Sacramento Record Union, January 16, 1897

San Francisco Call, June 26, 1902

San Francisco Call, June 6, 1909

San Francisco Call, March 10, 1920

San Francisco Call, October 18, 1896

San Francisco Call, September 8, 1898

Santa Cruz Daily Sentinel, June 25, 1895

About the Author

Janice Oberding is a Nevada-based writer who was lucky enough to have grown up in both California (the Monterey Peninsula,) and Nevada (Reno). She enjoys traveling and researching history, true crime, and the paranormal. She is one of only a few people who have spent an entire night at Alcatraz—aside from those who were incarcerated there. She worked as consultant and historian for the Alcatraz episode of SyFy's *Ghost Hunters* (with Jason Hawes and Grant Wilson).

She has also worked with the History Channel, LivingTV, and the Travel Channel, and has appeared in episodes of *Dead Famous* for Twofour productions, Travel Channel's *Haunted Hotels*, *Ghost Adventures*, and Fox's *Scariest Places on Earth*.

Janice has previously published spooky books with Stackpole, Arcadia/History Press, Pelican Publishing, and Fonthill Publishing. When she's not writing, she teaches an annual ghost hunting 101 class for Truckee Meadows Community College's Paranormal Series. She also speaks at local events and paranormal conferences. Although she has had inexplicable things occur during her research, Janice remains a skeptic. You can find her online at facebook.com/JaniceOberding and Twitter, @JaniceOberding.